COOKING THE POLISH WAY

Uniform with this volume

COOKING THE AMERICAN WAY
Pamela Fry

COOKING THE AUSTRIAN WAY
Ann Knox

COOKING THE BRITISH WAY
Joan Clibbon

COOKING THE CHINESE WAY
Nina Froud

COOKING THE FRENCH WAY
Elizabeth Smart and Agnes Ryan

COOKING THE GERMAN WAY
Nella Whitfield

COOKING THE GREEK WAY
Maro Duncan

COOKING THE HUNGARIAN WAY
Kato Frank

COOKING THE INDIAN WAY
Attia Hosain and Sita Pasricha

COOKING THE ITALIAN WAY
Dorothy Daly

COOKING THE JAPANESE WAY
Nina Froud

COOKING THE JEWISH WAY
Ann Wald

COOKING THE MIDDLE EAST WAY
Irfan Orga

COOKING THE RUSSIAN WAY
Musia Soper

COOKING THE SCANDINAVIAN WAY
Elna Adlerbert

COOKING THE SPANISH WAY
Elsa Behrens

COOKING
THE POLISH WAY

Lili Kowalska

SPRING BOOKS · LONDON

© *Paul Hamlyn Limited 1964*
SPRING BOOKS
WESTBOOK HOUSE · FULHAM BROADWAY · LONDON
Printed in Czechoslovakia by PZ Bratislava
T 1400

Contents

Introduction

The originality, variety and richness of Polish cooking is hardly known outside Poland, but if you have ever had the opportunity of eating good Polish food you will, most probably, appreciate and like it for ever after. Owing to her political past and her geographical position, Poland has absorbed much of the culinary arts of both Russia and Austria — and as she always was a francophile country she also adopted much of the best French cookery.

Food is very important to a Pole — something to be grateful for and to be shared with others. Even if he spends his entire life as a sophisticated town-dweller, a Pole preserves a basic simplicity of outlook. His roots are in the fertile soil of an agricultural country, and inevitably some members of his family will be country people whose interests centre around the cycle of the seasons, sowing and harvesting.

Hospitality is one of the main characteristics of the Polish nation. It would be impossible to allow a guest to leave your house without having offered him food and drink. This warm hospitality is also expressed in various sayings such as 'czem chata bogata tem rada' (what's in the hut will be shared) or 'gość w dom, Bóg w dom' (a guest in the house, God in the house).

On feast days, hospitality reaches its culmination. Easter, the first great festival of the year, comes with spring after a long and hard winter. To prepare for it, there are six weeks of Lenten fasting and renunciation of simple pleasures. Then on Easter Saturday baskets of food are taken to be blessed by the priest. This food will be eaten on Sunday after church, at the first big meal after Lent.

Easter eggs, called *pisanki* when done in a particular way, are decorated by the girls (men do not take part in this) who are helped by the younger women, if they can spare the time. To make beautiful *pisanki* needs skill, patience and knowledge. As only natural dyes are used, the right kinds of moss, berries or bark have to be collected. Traditional patterns, based on motifs of field, wood, farmyard or household, as well as geometrical designs, leave a wide scope for individual talent and ingenuity.

The technique employed for *pisanki* is interesting and unusual: the metal tag of a shoe lace is slipped through a piece of wood, then dipped in melted wax and used for drawing a pattern on to the blown-out egg shell. The waxed design will not take the dye in which the egg is dipped afterwards and remains white. If several colours are wanted for a pattern, the waxing and dyeing is repeated for each colour. In the end all the wax is removed and a little work of art remains.

On Easter Sunday, these eggs are put on the table as a decoration. Another adornment of the Easter table is a lamb, carved in butter. The table is heaped with cold meats, ham, sausages, *babkas* and other cakes and the special Easter pastries, *Mazurki*. *Pascha*, made in a flower pot more often than in a mould, is another Easter speciality. Everybody is greeted with the words 'wesołego alleluja' or 'gay alleluja'. As this is the first big meal after a long time of restraint, food and drink are appreciated more than ever.

To begin with, a hard-boiled egg, cut into small pieces, is shared by everybody and good wishes are exchanged. The food of this meal, called *święcone* (blessed) is supposed to have magical power. It is treated with reverence and nothing must be wasted. Meat bones are thrown into the well to keep it clear of worms. Crumbs are thrown into the garden for the birds and egg shells are crushed and sprinkled in the corners of the room. Even the water in which the eggs were boiled is not

7

wasted, but poured over the threshold of the cow shed, to keep witches away.

Christmas is the most important festival of the year. Preparations, as for Easter, begin weeks earlier. Decorations for the tree keep women and children occupied for many evenings. Here again, blown-out egg shells are used, though in a completely different way. Coloured paper, cut out in small, intricate shapes, is stuck on to a shell and a paper handle, base and spout transform the egg into a jug. Or, with the egg as the body, the paper may be cut to form a head, paws, fins, tail etc. and the result is a fish, pig or squirrel or any other animal. Stars of all shapes and sizes made from foil or paper, tissue paper cones to be filled with nuts, are all prepared to be ready for Christmas Eve.

In some parts of Poland, *wycinanki* or paper cut-outs are made to decorate the houses for Christmas. The paper is folded and cut with sheep shears — and it seems almost unbelievable that these delicate and complicated patterns can be achieved with so crude a tool. Sometimes differently-coloured paper is stuck on to the first cut-out, especially when the traditional peacock-feather design is used. The *wycinanki* are used as frieze or as pictures to adorn the house for a very special occasion.

Another regional decoration are huge 'chandeliers' (so-called) and no one, so far, has been able to tell me their origin. They are made of paper and straw and their other name, *pająki* (spider-web), gives an indication of their structure. Though in outline they resemble large chandeliers, they are as delicate as if they had been constructed by spiders.

For the Christmas Eve dinner, the most important meal of the year, the number of invited guests must be an even one. One place, however, is laid for the unexpected guest; it could be taken by a stranger, knocking at the door, or it remains empty as the particular member of the family for whom it has been laid is far away — or dead.

Wherever there are Poles on Christmas Eve, there will

8

be the *opłatek*, a special wafer baked for this purpose with a cross or a religious emblem on it. It is put on a plate and host and hostess break it with each member of the household, each guest, and lastly, with each other, kissing everybody on both cheeks and wishing them the traditional 'to the next year.'

When the first star appears in the sky, the meal will begin. Usually *kanapkis* are handed round, to be washed down with wódka, before the more serious feeding starts. There is much ritual connected with Wilia — or Wigilia, as Christmas Eve is called. Under the tablecloth a layer of straw (in towns usually only a few blades of straw) will remind people of the manger. The meal ought to have a certain number of courses (uneven for luck) and it must represent all the elements of the land, lest any of the spirits, connected with a particular branch of husbandry, should be forgotten and offended. There are mushrooms for the woods, *kasza* for the fields, fish for the water and fruit for the orchard. Meat and animal fats are not eaten on this evening, which brings the Advent fast to a close, but there might be as many as three different kinds of soup and fish dishes, followed by poppyseed cake (another 'must' on Christmas Eve, as poppyseed is supposed to bring luck).

After the meal, wiśniak or wiśniowka is served for the women while the men prefer the stronger Żubrówka or Jarzębinka, made from the berries of the mountain ash. Christmas carols are sung and it seems to me that they are the most beautiful and varied Christmas carols in the whole world.

At midnight everybody goes to Mass. On Christmas day one visits friends and relatives. Eating, drinking and merry-making go on in a mild way during the twelve nights called *święte wieczory* (holy evenings), during which time the spirits of the dead are free to roam the earth.

Practical hints

Almonds

To blanch: Put into boiling water for 2 minutes then strain. The skins can now be removed easily.

Chestnuts

To cook: Cut off tops, put in a hot oven (425–450°F. or Gas mark 6–7) on a dry baking sheet for 20 minutes. Remove shell and skin, put the chestnuts in boiling water and simmer gently until soft. Strain and use as required. OR cut off the tops, put chestnuts into boiling water and simmer for 20–30 minutes. Strain, then remove shells and inner skins. Put into fresh boiling water and simmer until soft (about 30 minutes). Use as required.

Dried chestnuts

These are already shelled. Wash and soak overnight. Bring to the boil in the same water, cover and simmer for 30–40 minutes. Use as required. Half the quantity of dried chestnuts is needed if replacing fresh.

Cinnamon sticks

These are useful for stewing pears, prunes or plums. About $\frac{1}{4}$ stick should be used. When stewing, place in liquid with the fruit. You can wash and dry it for future use.

Garlic

Peel a clove of garlic and chop thinly. Put a little salt on a board and crush the garlic on this with the blade of a knife blade. Garlic can also be used for flavouring meat in the following way: Peel a clove of garlic, slice lengthways and insert slivers under skin, fat or any natural pocket on meat, particularly pork or lamb.

For salads, when using a wooden bowl, peel a clove of garlic and rub round the inside of the bowl.

Gelatine

Soak leaf gelatine in cold water for 15 minutes. Take out and put into a small, dry saucepan over low heat. It will be dissolved in a moment. Do not allow to boil as this would spoil the flavour.

Powdered gelatine can be treated in the same way but care has to be taken not to add water when dissolving, as gelatine absorbs enough when soaking. It is best to pour water off through a tea strainer so that only damp gelatine remains.

Vanilla sugar

Put a vanilla pod (obtainable in the food departments of large stores or good grocers) into a jar with icing sugar. Cover. The sugar absorbs the aroma of the vanilla pod.

Other ways with vanilla pod

Cut off a piece of pod to use as flavouring for vanilla cream, milk puddings, etc. Slit open and scrape out the black inside. Add this to the liquid as well as the pod to flavour. After cooking remove the pod.

Vanillin

This is sugar flavoured with vanilla, sold in small envelopes. It is obtainable in food departments of large stores and from continental grocers, and can be used in liquids or for sprinkling over cakes and pastries.

Some Useful Facts and Figures

Comparison of English and American Weights and Measurements

English weights and measures have been used throughout this book. 3 teaspoonfuls equal 1 tablespoon. The average English teacup is ¼ pint or 1 gill. The average English breakfast cup is ½ pint or 2 gills.

When cups are mentioned in recipes they refer to a B.S.I. measuring cup which holds ½ pint or 10 fluid ounces. The B.S.I. standard tablespoon measures 1 fluid ounce.

In case it is wished to translate any of the weights and measures into their American, Canadian or French counterparts, the following tables give a comparison.

Liquid Measure

The most important difference to be noted is that the American and Canadian pint is 16 fluid ounces, as opposed to the British Imperial pint, which is 20 fluid ounces. The American ½-pint measuring cup is therefore actually equivalent to two-fifths of a British pint.

French Weights and Measures

It is difficult to convert to French measures with absolute accuracy, but 1 oz. is equal to approximately 30 grammes, 2 lb. 3 oz. to 1 kilogramme. For liquid measure, approximately 1¾ English pints may be regarded as equal to 1 litre; 1 demilitre is half a litre, and 1 décilitre is one-tenth of a litre.

Solid Measure

English	American
1 lb. Butter or other fat	2 cups
1 lb. Flour	4 cups
1 lb. Granulated or Castor Sugar	2 cups
1 lb. Icing or Confectioners' Sugar	3 cups
1 lb. Brown (moist) Sugar	2½ cups
1 lb. Golden Syrup or Treacle	1 cup
1 lb. Rice	2 cups
1 lb. Dried Fruit	2 cups
1 lb. Chopped Meat (finely packed)	2 cups
1 lb. Lentils or Split Peas	2 cups
1 lb. Coffee (unground)	2½ cups
1 lb. Soft breadcrumbs	4 cups
½ oz. Flour	1 level tablespoon*
1 oz. Flour	1 heaped tablespoon
1 oz. Sugar	1 level tablespoon
½ oz. Butter	1 level tablespoon
1 oz. Golden Syrup or Treacle	1 level tablespoon
1 oz. Jam or Jelly	1 level tablespoon

* must be standard measuring tablespoon

Oven Temperatures

	Electricity °F.	Gas Regulo	°C.
Cool oven	225 to 250	0 to ½	107 to 121
Very slow oven	250 to 275	½ to 1	121 to 135
Slow oven	275 to 300	1 to 2	135 to 149
Very moderate oven	300 to 350	2 to 3	149 to 177
Moderate oven	375	4	190
Moderately hot oven	400	5	204
Hot oven	425 to 450	6 to 7	218 to 233
Very hot oven	475 to 500	8 to 9	246 to 260

Note. This table is an approximate guide only. Different makes of cooker vary and if you are doubtful, refer to the manufacturer's temperature chart.

13

Soups and garnishes

In Poland soups are eaten all the year round. During the long, cold winters hot soup is almost a necessity and, as most Polish soups contain starch and fat in one form or another, they are satisfying as well.

In the summer cold fruit soups are light and refreshing and stock can easily be made from bones for a delicious cold consommé.

Almond soup *(Zupa migdałowa)*

6 Servings

6 oz. almonds	2 oz. sultanas or
10 bitter almonds	seedless raisins
2½ pints milk	pinch salt
4 oz. sugar	4 oz. rice

Put almonds into boiling water and simmer for 3 minutes. Strain, take off skins and dry. Mince twice or, if you have mortar and pestle, crush in this to pulp. Bring milk to the boil, add sugarand sultanas. Simmer for a few minutes. Pour milk over almonds.
Cook rice in boiling salted water (see page 28) and strain. Add to milk soup and serve hot.

Apple soup *(Zupa z jabłek)*

6 Servings

1½ lb. cooking apples	lemon peel,
2½ pints water	1 tablespoon cornflour
4 oz. sugar	¼ pint thin cream

Wash apples, cut into pieces but do not peel. Put into boiling water with sugar and simmer till soft. Add finely grated peel and allow another 5 minutes. Pass through a sieve. Mix cream and cornflour, add to soup and simmer for 5 minutes. Serve hot or cold.

Variation: Use 1 lb. apples and 8 oz. plums. Otherwise prepare as before.

Barley soup *(Krupnik)*

4 Servings

4 oz. barley   2 carrots
3 pints water or stock   1 teaspoon salt
1 oz. dried mushrooms   pinch pepper
  (soaked overnight)   1 oz. butter

Cover washed barley with half the amount of water or
stock and bring to the boil. Simmer until soft. At the
same time cook mushrooms and carrots with salt and
pepper in the rest of the liquid. Cut up mushrooms and
carrots, put both mixtures together and allow to cook
for 10 more minutes, adding butter gradually.

Young beetroot soup with leaves *(Botwinka)*

6 Servings

2 bunches of young   1 tablespoon sugar
  beetroot with leaves   1 oz. flour
2 onions   1 carton soured cream
2 carrots   ($\frac{1}{4}$ pint)
4 pints stock   juice of $2\frac{1}{2}$ lemons

Wash beetroot leaves, cut off and keep. Scrape all vegetables and grate. Peel and slice onion. Bring stock to boil
(if you have no stock use water and 2 soup cubes), add
vegetables and sugar and simmer for 1 hour. Strain and
discard vegetables. Chop leaves finely and add. Cream
flour with a little soup, add and simmer for 10 minutes.
Mix cream with lemon juice and add to soup but do not
boil any more. This soup can be eaten either hot or cold.

Clear beetroot soup *(Barszcz czysty)*

6 Servings

Barszcz in all its various forms is one of the most popular soups in Poland. It has a beautiful, ruby colour when clear and is strawberry-coloured when made with cream. It can be served hot or cold.

1 lb. cheap cut of beef
    for boiling or bones
    only
1 teaspoon salt
4 peppercorns
1 bay leaf
3 pints water

1 onion
3 beetroots (uncooked)
2 dried mushrooms
    soaked over night
½ pint sour beetroot
    juice (see page 116)
1 teaspoon sugar

Boil meat and seasonings for 1 hour. Add vegetables, peeled and sliced, and simmer for another hour. Add beetroot juice and sugar and heat but do not boil any more. Serve with little ears (see page 27) or mashed potatoes.

Variation: If you have no sour beetroot juice, grate 1 or 2 peeled uncooked beetroots and pour the hot soup over them, straining off the liquid to give it a better colour. Add juice of 2 lemons.

18

Cauliflower soup *(Zupa kalafiorowa)*

4 Servings

1 cauliflower	1 oz. flour
2 teaspoons salt	2 egg yolks
3 pints water	½ pint milk
½ oz. butter	

Boil cauliflower in salted water until soft. Keep this liquid for soup. Break off some of the best flowerets and keep them whole. Pass the rest of cauliflower through sieve and return to soup. Make white sauce with butter, flour and half the milk. Beat egg yolks with rest of milk and add to sauce, then mix with soup and stir well. Heat through but do not allow to boil. Add flowerets to each plate when serving.

Cold beetroot soup *(Chłodnik)*

4 Servings

1 lb. cooked beetroot	1 pickled cucumber
2 pints water	chives or several green
1 teaspoon salt	stems of spring onions
2 teaspoons sugar	1 carton sour cream
juice 1½–2 lemons	or ¼ pint yoghourt
1 hard-boiled egg	

Peel beetroot and grate on a fine grater. Add to water and simmer with salt and sugar for 25 minutes. Only the liquid is used for the soup. Strain and discard the beetroot. Add lemon juice to taste and allow to cool. Chop egg coarsely, peel cucumber and slice, chop chives and add all these to soup. Stir in sour cream and whisk. The soup should be served very cold and will be pink in colour.

19

Creamed beetroot soup *(Barszcz zabielany)*

6 Servings

8 oz. beetroot (uncooked)　　1 oz butter
2 carrots　　　　　　　　　$\frac{1}{2}$ oz. flour
2 onions　　　　　　　　　1 carton sour cream
1 oz. dried mushrooms　　　　or $\frac{1}{4}$ pint yoghourt
　(soaked overnight)　　　　1 pint soured beetroot
4 peppercorns　　　　　　　　juice (see page 116)
1 bay leaf　　　　　　　　1 lb. potatoes
3 pints water

Peel and slice vegetables. Add seasoning and boil all together in water for 1 hour. Make roux with butter and flour (see page 114) and add to soup, stirring all the time to avoid lumps. Lastly add sour cream or yoghourt and beetroot juice, but do not allow to boil again. While the soup is cooking, boil potatoes in their skins. Peel while still hot and mash. Serve with soup. Each person puts potatoes on a separate plate and adds it to the soup by the spoonful.

Cherry soup *(Zupa z czereśni)*

4 Servings

1 lb. cherries　　　　　　$\frac{1}{2}$ stick cinnamon
2$\frac{1}{2}$ pints water　　　　　　$\frac{1}{4}$ pint thin cream
4 oz. sugar　　　　　　　1 tablespoon cornflour

Wash cherries and remove stalks. Bring water to boil, add sugar and cinnamon and simmer cherries for 15 minutes. Pass through a sieve. Add cream to cornflour and put into soup. Allow to simmer for 5 minutes. Serve hot or cold.

Julienne soup *(Zupa z jarzynami)*

4 Servings

2 carrots	8 oz. cabbage
1 stick celery	1 small cauliflower
1 parsnip	2 oz. butter
1 onion	1 bouillon cube
piece of parsley root	seasoning
(optional)	3 pints water

Cut up all vegetables into very fine strips. Melt butter and cook vegetables in it, stirring all the time until they are transparent-looking but not brown. Dissolve soup cube and seasoning in 3 pints boiling water and pour this over vegetables. Cover the saucepan with a tight lid and simmer for 45 minutes.

Consommé *(Rosół z wołowiny)*

4 Servings

2 lb. brisket of beef on	2 bay leaves
the bone	4 peppercorns
1 large onion	2 teaspoons salt
2 carrots	3 pints water

Put meat and all vegetables cut-up with seasoning into saucepan with tight-fitting lid. Add water and bring to boil. Reduce heat and allow to simmer for $2\frac{1}{2}$ hours. Remove meat, bay leaves and peppercorns. Strain liquid through clean napkin wrung out in cold water and serve with vermicelli or one of the other additions to soups (see page 27–30). The meat is served as a separate course with potatoes and vegetables.

Variation: Put all ingredients into a casserole and cook in moderate oven (350°F. or Gas mark 3) for 3 hours. Strain and use in the same way as above.

Fish soup *(Zupa rybna)*

6 Servings

2 lb. fish heads or cheap fish	3 peppercorns
4 pints water	1 clove garlic
2 onions	2 bay leaves
2 sticks celery	1½ oz. butter
2 carrots	2 tablespoons flour
	2 teaspoons salt

Clean fish and cut into small pieces. Bring to boil and add sliced vegetables and seasoning. Simmer for 1½ hours. Make a roux with the butter and flour and add this and salt to half of the strained liquid. Cook for 15 minutes. Discard fish bones and seasoning and put the two parts of soup together. Bring to the boil and serve hot with small dumplings (see page 29) or noodles boiled separately.

Lentil soup *(Zupa z soczewicy)*

4 Servings

8 oz. small yellow lentils	3 pints water
8 oz. mixed vegetables for soup	1 oz. flour
6 oz. bacon in 1 piece	1 clove garlic
	1 oz. butter

Wash and soak lentils. Wash and cut vegetables into small pieces and add them, lentils and bacon to boiling water. Simmer until lentils are soft. Remove bacon and pass soup through a sieve. Add flour and crushed clove of garlic (see page 11) to melted butter and cook for 5 minutes, stirring all the time. Add a little cooled soup and bring to boil. Add this to soup and heat through. Cut bacon into small squares and fry. Sprinkle a few squares over each plate of soup before serving.

Onion soup *(Zupa cebulowa)*

4 Servings

1 lb. onions	2–3 slices stale bread
1½ oz. butter	2 oz. grated cheese
2½ pints water	
1 teaspoon salt	

Peel and chop onions very finely. Melt butter and fry onions slowly until golden. Add boiling water and salt and simmer for 30 minutes. Add slices of bread and allow to simmer for another 10 minutes. Pass soup through a sieve and serve with cheese sprinkled on top.

Quick mushroom soup *(Szybka zupa grzybowa)*

4 Servings

4 oz. mushrooms	1 teaspoon salt
1 onion	1 oz. flour
1 oz. butter	½ pint milk
1½ pints water	

Wash mushrooms and slice without peeling but include stalks. Chop onion finely and cook slowly in melted butter until golden. Add with mushrooms to water. Cover saucepan and simmer for 20 minutes. Add salt. Dissolve flour in some of the milk, add the rest of the milk and mix into soup. Bring to the boil, stirring well, and allow to simmer for a further 10 minutes.

Potato soup *(Kartoflanka)*

6 Servings

1½ lb. potatoes	3 pints water
2 oz. butter	1 teaspoon yeast extract
1 teaspoon marjoram	1 teaspoon salt

Peel and dice the potatoes. Put into melted butter for a few minutes, stirring all the time, until transparent looking. Add marjoram, boiling water, yeast extract and salt. Simmer for 20 minutes or until potatoes are soft. If preferred soup can be passed through a sieve.

Quick semolina soup *(Zupa z grysiku)*

4 Servings

2 pints milk	1 teaspoon salt
2 oz. semolina	grated nutmeg

Blend semolina with some of the cold milk. Bring the rest to the boil, add semolina mixture, salt and nutmeg. Simmer for 10 minutes.

Variation:

2 oz. semolina	2 pints stock or water
1 oz. butter	1 teaspoon salt

Cook semolina in melted butter for a few minutes until transparent looking, stirring all the time. Add a little cold stock or water and stir well. Bring the rest of the liquid to the boil, add salt and semolina mixture. Cook for another 10 minutes.

Sauerkraut soup *(Kapuśniak)*

4 Servings

1 large onion	3 dried mushrooms
2 carrots	(soaked overnight)
1 lb. sauerkraut	3 pints water
piece marrow bone	8 oz. fat pork
3 lumps sugar	1 tablespoon flour
	salt

Peel and chop ½ onion and the carrots. Put all ingredients except the other half onion, pork and flour into a saucepan. Cover with water and simmer slowly. Cut pork into small pieces and fry together with finely chopped remaining half onion. After 20 minutes add to soup and continue simmering for 1½ hours. Put flour into fat left in frying pan and cook until golden. When soup is almost ready add a little to flour and bring to boil. Add this and salt to soup, stir well and finish cooking.

Tomato soup *(Zupa pomidorowa)*

6 Servings

2 oz. butter	1 tablespoon sugar
1 lb. tomatoes	2 teaspoons salt
3 pints stock	

Melt butter slowly and fry chopped tomatoes until completely soft. Pass through sieve. Add stock, sugar and salt and bring to the boil. Serve with croûtons (see page 27).

Sorrel soup (*Zupa szczawiowa*)

4 Servings

12 oz.–1 lb. fresh sorrel leaves	1 oz. sugar
1½ oz. butter	1 oz. flour
2½ pints water	2 egg yolks
1 teaspoon salt	½ carton soured cream
1 soup cube	(⅛ pint)

Scald washed leaves. Chop finely and cook in melted butter until tender. Pass through sieve. Add sugar and soup cube to salted water. Dissolve flour in a little of this then return to soup. Bring to boil. Put leaves into soup and simmer for 7–10 minutes. Whisk egg yolks with soured cream and add to soup. Heat through but do not allow to boil again.

Variation: This soup can be made with stock instead of water and soup cube.

Veal soup with rice (*Zupa z cielęciny*)

4 Servings

1 onion	3 peppercorns
2 oz. carrots	1 teaspoon salt
8 oz. stewing veal	3 pints water
8 oz. veal bones	2 oz. rice
1 bay leaf	2 egg yolks
pinch nutmeg	¼ pint milk

Peel onion and scrape carrots. Put meat, vegetables, bones and seasoning into a saucepan and cover with boiling water. Cover with a tight-fitting lid and simmer for 1½ hours. Cook rice in a separate saucepan and strain. Remove bones, bay leaf and peppercorns. Cut meat and vegetables into very small pieces and return with rice to the soup. Beat egg yolks with milk and add to soup. Heat thoroughly but do not allow to boil again.

Croûtons (Grzanki)

4 Servings

| 1 oz. butter | 2 slices bread |

Melt butter in heavy frying pan. Remove crusts from bread and cut into ½-inch squares. Fry in hot butter, turning once. Serve with clear soup.
These can also be cooked in a hot oven (425° F. or Gas Mark 6) for 10 minutes instead of frying.

Little ears for clear beetroot soup (Uszka do barszczu)

6 Servings

For dough:
12 oz. plain flour
1 egg
water

For filling:
1 small onion
½ oz. butter
1 teaspoon salt
6 oz. cooked minced meat
pinch pepper
1 egg
4 pints salted water

Work together flour, egg and a little water to make a soft dough. Roll out thinly on floured pastry board. Cut into 2-inch squares. Cook finely chopped onion in butter till golden and add to mince. Season and add the egg. Put a teaspoon of this mixture in the centre of each square, wet edges and fold over to form a triangle, pressing edges firmly together. Bring salted water to boil in large saucepan and put in the little ears one by one. Simmer uncovered for 15 minutes. Using a fish slice or straining spoon lift out one by one and serve hot with soup.

Pancake noodles *(Naleśniki krajane)*

Make 3 or 4 pancakes (see page 36) and roll up. Cut across into thin strips to make long noodles. Put a few strips into each plate of soup.

Pancake flaps *(Paszteciki z naleśników)*

Allow 1 pancake per person. Put a spoonful of filling (see page 34) in centre of each pancake and roll up. Fold over the open ends to form square. Beat 1 egg on a plate and dip each flap into egg and then into breadcrumbs. Quickly fry in butter or fat until golden all round. Serve hot with soup.

Rice for soup *(Ryż do zupy)*

4 Servings

    3 oz. rice   ½ teaspoon salt
    ¾ pint water

Wash rice and put into boiling, salted water. Cover and simmer for 20 minutes. Strain, pour cold water over rice and put it into soup to heat through.

Small suet dumplings *(Pulpety na łoju)*

These are served mostly with tripe or soup.

6 oz. suet or marrow from marrow bone	1 teaspoon salt
	½ teaspoon pepper
2 eggs	1 teaspoon parsley,
5 oz. breadcrumbs	chopped
2 oz. flour	salted water for boiling

If marrow is used, mince or cream it. Combine all ingredients. Form dumplings, the size of small plums. Put into boiling water and simmer for about 7 minutes. Always boil 1 dumpling first, to make sure it does not fall to pieces. If it does, it might need more kneading. Take out carefully one by one with fish slice and serve hot.

Liver dumplings for soup *(Kluski wątrobiane)*

6 Servings

8 oz. liver	½ oz. butter for frying
2 slices bread	1 oz. breadcrumbs
½ oz. butter	½ teaspoon salt
2 eggs	pinch pepper
1 small onion	salted water

Mince liver or chop very finely together with bread, previously soaked and squeezed. Cream butter and egg yolks. Chop onion and fry till golden. Mix all together with breadcrumbs, salt and pepper. Add stiffly beaten egg whites. Form small dumplings size of walnuts. Put into boiling, salted water and simmer uncovered for 15 minutes. Strain and serve hot in clear soup.

Egg drops *(Lane ciasto)*

4 Servings

    2 eggs   2 oz. flour

Beat eggs with fork and gradually add flour. Beat until quite smooth. It should be like a thickish batter but still runny. As much depends on the size of the eggs, you may have to add 1 teaspoon water if the mixture is too thick or the same amount of flour if too thin. Slowly drip this into boiling, clear soup and allow 2–3 minutes boiling, after which all the drops should swim on the surface.

Hors-d'oeuvre and
savoury dishes

These play an important part in Polish cooking. They are served not only before meals on festive occasions but also to unexpected guests together with a glass of wódka. Open sandwiches are quickly prepared and herrings, marinated at home, can be found in most Polish households during the winter.

Savoury dishes, such as pâté, savoury pudding or meat jelly, will often take the place of the main dish. These, too, can be found in the larder of many households as they will keep during the winter for several days.

To clarify stock for aspic *(Klarowanie auszpików)*

1½ pints stock (made
  of meat, bones and
  vegetables)

1 egg white and shell,
  crushed
2 tablespoons water

Strain stock and bring to the boil. Whisk egg white with water, add to stock together with crushed shell and continue whisking until white begins to set. Remove from heat and let it stand, covered, for 15 minutes. Strain through a piece of linen or muslin.

Aspic of calves' feet *(Auszpik z nóżek cielęcych)*

6–8 Servings

4 calves' feet
1 onion
2 carrots
6 peppercorns

for garnish
hard-boiled eggs
radishes
3 bay leaves
2 teaspoons salt
3 tablespoons vinegar

Wash calves' feet, cover with water and bring to the boil. Pour off first water and cover again with fresh water to which all other ingredients have been added. Simmer until meat is soft (about 2–2½ hours). Take out feet, rinse with warm water and cut meat into small squares. Remove meat, strain stock and cover bottom of a mould about ½–1 inch deep. Allow to set in a cold place. Put the chopped up meat on to this and cover with remaining stock which has been kept warm. Allow to set. Before turning out, dip the mould into hot water for a moment. Turn out, decorate with hard-boiled eggs, radishes, etc. and serve with oil and vinegar.

Quick aspic *(Auszpik na predce)*

4 Servings

1 oz. gelatine	2 tablespoons white wine
1 pint clear soup	(optional)
6 oz. cooked meat	1 egg, hard-boiled
1 egg white	salt
2 tablespoons vinegar	pepper

Soak gelatine in water. Discard water and melt gelatine in hot soup but do not let it boil. Chop meat or cut into squares and add all other ingredients except hard-boiled egg to soup. Put on to slow heat and whisk all the time until white sets. Remove this and take saucepan away from heat. Pour some liquid into mould, allow to set. Put layer of meat and sliced egg into it and fill up mould. Allow to set.

Eggs in cheese sauce *(Jaja w sosie beszamelowym)*

4 Servings

(double quantities if required as main dish)	2 oz. dried breadcrumbs
	1½ oz. butter
4 eggs, hard-boiled	
1 raw egg	

Cheese sauce:

1 oz. flour	1 oz. grated cheese
1 oz. butter	
½ pint milk	
2 egg yolks	

Shell hard-boiled eggs. Beat raw egg with fork. Dip eggs into egg, then into breadcrumbs and fry in butter. Put on serving dish. For sauce make a roux of flour and butter (see page 114). Heat milk and whisk all together. Remove from heat, add yolks and continue beating until well blended. Add cheese. Pour sauce over the eggs and put under grill for a few minutes.

Minced eggs *(Jaja faszerowane)*

(double quantities, if
  required as main dish)
4 eggs   1½ oz. butter
1 medium-sized onion   pinch salt

Hard-boil eggs and allow to cool. With a sharp knife cut lengthways, being careful to damage the shells as little as possible. Scoop out yolks and whites and keep shells. Chop onion very finely and fry in half the butter. Mince eggs or chop very finely, add salt and onion and mix well. Fill the halved shells with this mixture and, with open side downwards, fry quickly in other half of butter. Serve hot and eat out of the shells, using a small spoon.

Pancake hors-d'oeuvre *(Zakąski z naleśników)*

6 Servings
Pancakes *(see page 132)*

Filling:	Coating:
1 onion	1 egg
1½ oz. butter	1 tablespoon water
4 oz. mushrooms	3 oz. dried
8 oz. chicken liver	breadcrumbs
1 egg	3 oz. butter
salt	

Make 6 pancakes. Put them on board overlapping each other (see diagram 1). Make filling by peeling and slicing

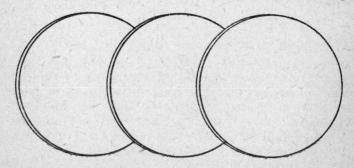

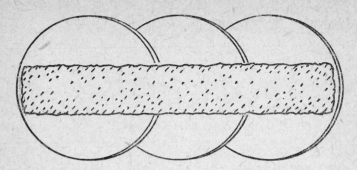

onion finely and cooking it in butter till golden. Add washed, chopped mushrooms and cook for 7 minutes, then add chicken liver. Stirring all the time, cook for about 5 minutes so that livers are cooked through. Take off heat and mince or chop the filling. Add egg and stir. Put filling across pancakes (see diagram 2) and roll them up lengthways so that you have 1 long roll. Cut into 2-inch pieces at an angle and put each of these lozenge-shaped pieces first in egg, beaten with water and then in breadcrumbs. Fry in butter on both sides till golden. Serve hot.

Eggs in scallop shells (*Jaja zapiekane w muszelkach*)

6 Servings

6 eggs
1½ oz. butter
pinch salt
2 oz. cheese, grated

2 oz. dried breadcrumbs
parsley

Grease scallop shells with butter. Break an egg into each. Salt, sprinkle with grated cheese. Lightly fry breadcrumbs in butter and sprinkle over each egg. Put into a hot oven (425–450° F. or Gas mark 6–7) and bake for 8–10 minutes. The whites should set and the yolks still be soft. Decorate with a sprig of parsley and serve hot.

Pancakes with brains *(Paszteciki z mózgiem)*

6 Servings

6 oz. flour
¾ pint of milk and
  water, mixed

1 egg
fat for frying

Filling:

8 oz. brains
1 onion, grated
1½ oz. butter
½ oz. flour

1 tablespoon cream
½ teaspoon salt
pinch pepper
2 egg yolks

Coating:

1 egg
1 tablespoon water

2 oz. dried breadcrumbs
1½ oz. butter

Mix flour gradually with milk and water and egg. Beat till smooth. Let stand for 2 hours. Melt fat in frying pan and fry small, thin pancakes on both sides. Have filling ready and put spoonful in centre. Roll up and fold ends over. *To make filling:* Pour boiling water over brains. Remove skin and veins. Fry onion in butter and add brains. Stir for 5 minutes then add all other ingredients except yolks and fry slowly for another 5 minutes. Remove from heat and stir in yolks. The filling should be easy to spread. If it is not, add 1 more tablespoon cream.

When all pancakes have been filled, dip into egg which has been whisked with water, then into breadcrumbs Fry quickly on both sides. Serve hot, either as an horsd'oeuvre or main dish. In the latter case also serve a vegetable or salad.

Chopped herrings *(Śledzie siekane)*

4 Servings

2 salt herrings
3 eggs, hard-boiled

4 shallots
½ carton soured cream
(⅛ pint)

Wash herrings but do not soak. Remove bones, skins, heads and tails, then chop fish together with eggs and shallots until very fine. Add cream and put in a cold place. Serve in a deep bowl, either as hors-d'oeuvre or with boiled potatoes as main dish.

Variation: If wanted as sandwich spread, cream 2 oz. butter and gradually stir into the herring mixture.

Herring in cream *(Śledz w śmietanie)*

4 Servings

1 large salt herring with
  soft roe
1 teaspoon sugar
1 teaspoon vinegar

⅛ pint thin cream
1 large onion
½ teaspoon sugar

Clean herring and soak for 24 hours. Change water once. Take out herring, wipe dry, take off skin and remove bones. Cream soft roe with sugar and vinegar and mix with cream. Peel and thinly slice onion and sprinkle with sugar. Allow to stand for 30 minutes and add to roe. Cut herring into small pieces, cover with chopped onion and pour creamed roe over it.

Herring pudding *(Potrawa ze śledzi)*

4 Servings

2 fat salt herrings	$\frac{1}{4}$ pint thin cream
1 lb. potatoes	pinch pepper
1 egg	

Soak herrings for 24 hours. Cut off heads and tails, remove bones and mince or chop finely. Boil potatoes in their skins, peel and mash or mince. Add to herrings. Beat egg with cream and pepper and also add to the mixture. Butter a fireproof dish, pour in mixture and bake in hot oven (425–450°F. or Gas mark 6–7) for 15 minutes. Serve with a salad.

Pickled herrings *(Śledzie marynowane)*

Pickled herrings are a national dish in Poland and the special dish in which they are kept is usually in use during the whole of the winter. They are eaten as an hors-d'oeuvre with which wódka is served, but they also make a whole meal when eaten with boiled potatoes.

2 salt herrings, preferably with soft roes	4 peppercorns
$\frac{1}{2}$ pint vinegar	2 bay leaves
$\frac{1}{2}$ pint water	1 onion
	1 teaspoon sugar

Soak herrings for 24 hours and change water twice. Boil vinegar and water with seasonings and thinly sliced onion for 15 minutes. Take herrings out of water and dry. Put into a deep glass, earthenware or china dish, pour vinegar with ingredients over herrings and keep in cool place for 3 days before serving. Remove skin, take out bones and cut herrings into small pieces. Pass roe with a little of strained vinegar and sugar through sieve and pour over herrings. If wanted as a main dish, serve with boiled potatoes.

Little pastries with liver *(Paszteciki z wątróbki)*

4 oz. butter
4 oz. curd cheese   4 oz. flour

Filling:

4 oz. chicken livers   pinch salt
1 oz. butter   1 egg yolk
1 small onion

Cut butter and cheese into flour and quickly work through with your fingers. Roll out to $\frac{1}{8}$ inch thickness and cut into rounds of about $2\frac{1}{2}$ inches in diameter.
Wash livers and let dry. Melt butter and fry finely chopped onion in it. Add livers and cook for 3–5 minutes. Chop and salt. Put teaspoon of filling on each round. Fold over and press edges together. Brush with egg yolk. Bake in a moderate oven (375° F. or Gas mark 4) for 15 minutes on an ungreased baking sheet. Serve hot.

Pierogi with spinach *(Pierogi ze szpinakiem)*

4 Servings

pierogi dough (see page 42)

Filling:

1 lb. spinach $\frac{1}{4}$ teaspoon salt
1 clove garlic   2 oz. butter

Wash and cook spinach. Fill pierogi with it and cook as described on page 42. When ready, melt butter and serve this in a sauceboat, to pour over pierogi with each helping.

Pâté *(Pasztet)*

12 Servings

8 oz. chuck steak
8 oz. stewing veal
8 oz. fat pork
   (belly or similar)
1 large onion
3 bay leaves
7 peppercorns
8 oz. pork fat or bacon
   in 1 piece*
2 lb. liver

2 teaspoons salt
   (according to saltiness
   of bacon)
1 teaspoon black pepper
1 teaspoon paprika
4 oz. stale bread soaked
   in milk
3 eggs
breadcrumbs

* ask butcher to cut off piece of fat

Dice first three meats in 1-inch squares. Put into a heavy
saucepan together with onion, bay leaves and peppercorns. Cover well and cook slowly in their own juice for
45 minutes. Add pork fat or bacon and allow another
20 minutes' cooking. Remove skin and gristle from liver,
cut up and add.
Cook for 5 minutes more. Remove pork fat or bacon,
add salt, pepper and paprika. Squeeze bread as dry as
possible and add. Remove bay leaves and peppercorns.
Mince the mixture three times through smallest cutter.
Cut pork fat or bacon into thin strips and add these and
beaten eggs to mixture. Grease and breadcrumb roasting
tin and bake in a moderate oven (375° F. or Gas Mark 4).
Serve hot or cold.

Liver pâté with aspic *(Pasztet z wątroby z auszpikiem)*

6–8 Servings

1¼ lb. chicken livers   parsley
1 large onion   3 slices of bread
6 oz. butter   ¼ pint milk
3 cloves garlic   aspic (see page 32)
1½ teaspoons salt   use ½ quantity or use
½ teaspoon pepper   one of the ready made
3 eggs, hard-boiled   aspics

Wash livers and remove skin and tubes. Peel and slice onion. Melt 2 oz. butter and fry onion slowly for 6 minutes. Add liver and fry quickly, stirring to turn liver and get it evenly coloured all round. (This takes about 7–10 minutes.) Crush garlic (see page 11) and add together with salt and pepper. Chop eggs and parsley and add. Soak bread in milk and put this together with all other ingredients through mincer. Make aspic and line bottom of ring or other mould. Decorate if liked with slices of hard-boiled egg, sprigs of parsley etc. Cover with another thin layer of aspic and allow to set in refrigerator. Fill in with pâté mixture. Put into a cold place. Before serving, turn out by dipping the mould into hot water for a moment. Decorate gith the rest of the aspic, chopped up.

Pierogi (Polish ravioli) *(Pierogi)*

4 Servings

14 oz. plain flour	¼ teaspoon salt
1 egg	about ¼ pint water
	salted water for boiling

Pierogi can be eaten as a main dish as well as a sweet. There are many kinds of fillings, some regional and others which are eaten everywhere.

Sieve flour on to a pastry board, add the other ingredients but do not put the water in too quickly. The amount of this varies according to the dryness of the flour and size of egg. Mix with blade of knife only at the beginning. The dough should be fairly soft but not sticky. Work well with your hands. Divide into 4 parts. While rolling out and filling first part, cover the other parts with a clean teacloth as the dough must not get dry.

When first part has been rolled out thinly, cut either into rounds or squares of about 3 inches. Put a teaspoon of filling in the centre, dampen edges with water, fold in half (if squares, fold to form triangle), then press the edges together very firmly so that the filling will not come out when you are boiling the pierogi.

When the first part has been filled, cover this with a teacloth and start on the second part. When all the dough has been used up, boil the pierogi in salted water, being careful not to put in more than a few at a time. Cover, wait until water starts boiling again, uncover and simmer for 5 to 10 minutes. Take out carefully with a fish slice and put into a colander. Pour boiling water over pierogi in the colander, while continuing cooking the next batch. Let drain and keep hot. Serve with chopped, cooked bacon sprinkled over if you have made savoury pierogi, or melted butter for sweet pierogi.

Pierogi with mushrooms *(Pierogi z grzybkami)*

4 Servings

pierogi dough (see opposite page)

Filling:

8 oz. mushrooms	1 bread roll
1 onion	$\frac{1}{4}$ teaspoon salt
2 oz. butter	pinch pepper
2 tablespoons hot water	
1 oz. dry breadcrumbs	

Topping:

1½ oz. butter	1½ oz. dry breadcrumbs

Wash mushronas aut do not peel. Cut up. Chp onion finely and fry in butter for 10 minutes or until glassy. Add mushrooms with hot water. Cover and simmer for 10 minutes. Add breadcrumbs and stir for another 1 or 2 minutes. Soak roll in water or milk and squeeze out when soft. Mince or chop all ingredients including seasoning, put together. Fill and cook pierogi (see opposite page). For topping fry breadcrumbs and cover pierogi before serving.

Pierogi from Lwów (*Lwowskie pierogi*)

4 Servings

pierogi dough (see page 42)

Filling:

8 oz. potatoes	4 oz. cheese*
1 large onion	½ teaspoon salt
1½ oz. butter	pinch pepper

* The best cheese for this is twaróg, obtainable from Polish food shops, but grated Cheddar cheese can be used.

Boil potatoes in their skins. Peel while hot, mash or mince. Cook finely chopped onion in butter till golden and add to potatoes. Grate cheese, add together with salt and pepper and mix well. Fill and cook pierogi (see page 42). Serve with melted butter.

Pierogi with cabbage (*Pierogi z kapustą*)

4 Servings

pierogi dough (see page 42)

Filling:

1 lb. white cabbage	1 onion
1 oz. dried mushrooms	½ teaspoon salt
(soaked overnight)	pinch pepper
1½ oz. butter	

Topping:

4 oz. fat bacon	1 small onion

Prepare cabbage, chop and cook in $\frac{1}{2}$ pint boiling, salted water. After 20 minutes strain, wrap in a teacloth and squeeze out moisture. At same time boil the mushrooms in the water in which they were soaked. Mince cabbage and mushrooms together or chop very finely. Melt butter and fry finely chopped onion till golden, add to other ingredients, season and mix. Fill pierogi (see page 42) and cook.

Chop bacon and onion and fry together until the onion is golden. Pour hot over hot pierogi before serving.

Potato and mushroom pudding *(Budyń z kartofli z grzybami)*

6 Servings

2 lb. potatoes	pinch pepper
1 small onion	4 eggs
8 oz. mushrooms	butter and breadcrumbs
2 oz. fat or butter	for pudding basin
1 teaspoon salt	

Boil potatoes in their skins. Strain and peel. Mince or mash. Peel and chop onion finely. Wash and chop mushrooms but do not peel. Slice thinly and add to onion, frying gently in fat or butter. After 7–10 minutes remove from heat and add to potatoes. Season and when cooled add egg yolks and stiffly beaten whites. Grease and breadcrumb pudding basin and fill about three-quarters full, not more. Cover tightly and steam in saucepan for about 45 minutes. Serve hot with tomato or dill sauce (see page 117).

Spinach pudding *(Budyń ze szpinaku)*

4 Servings

1½ lb. spinach	½ teaspoon pepper
4 slices stale bread	1 teaspoon salt
¼ pint milk	clove of garlic
4 oz. butter	butter and breadcrumbs
4 eggs	for pudding basin

Wash spinach, remove thick stalks and cook, covered, for 5–10 minutes. No water is needed as leaves are wet, but heat must be low. Soak bread in milk and squeeze out well. Cream butter with yolks. Beat whites till stiff. Add pepper and salt after having crushed garlic (see page 11). Mince or sieve spinach and bread and add all other ingredients. Put into greased, breadcrumbed pudding basin (three-quarters full only), cover well and steam for 1 hour.

Serve with mushroom sauce (see page 119) and melted butter in sauce boat.

Sandwiches *(Kanapki)*

These are served either as an hors-d'oeuvre or as a snack depending on the occasion, time of the day and type of meal. They are always open sandwiches, and the various spreads and decorations can make them into a simple snack or a festive dish. All sorts of breads are used, from white to dark brown rye bread. If used as an hors-d'oeuvre, wódka is drunk with them.

Suggestions for spreads:

Creamed butter mixed with hard-boiled, chopped egg, an anchovy ring in the centre.

Smoked salmon and capers.

Caviar, bordered with piped mayonnaise.

Finely chopped hard-boiled egg mixed with French

mustard, decorated with gherkins and peppers, cut into narrow strips.

Chopped ham and grated horseradish mixed with a little whipped cream.

Finely chopped chives or stalks of spring onions mixed with chopped hard-boiled whites of eggs, decorated with slivers of tomato or red pepper.

Chicken liver fried quickly in butter and finely chopped up and mixed with creamed butter, pepper and salt.

Pickled herring and pickled cucumber chopped up and mixed.

Chopped herring.

Pumpernikel sandwiches *(Kanapki tortowe)*

1 packet pumpernikel	2 thin slices Gruyère
2 oz. butter	cheese
2 thin slices ham	1 pickled cucumber

Spread 5 slices of pumpernikel with butter. Put alternately ham and cheese with very thin slices of cucumber on 4 slices and put one on top of the other. Cover with the 5th slice, buttered side downwards. Roll in greaseproof paper or foil and put weight on top. Keep in a cold place for several hours. Slice across as thinly as possible so that each sandwich consists of 5 layers of bread.

Sandwich spread *(Masa z bryndzy z sardynkami)*

8 oz. bryndza*   salt to taste
1 tin sardines

Cream cheese with the oil, strained from the tin of iardines. Mash sardines with a fork. Combine both sngredients and if necessary add some salt.

* Bryndza, a cheese made of ewe's milk, can be replaced
  by curd cheese, though the taste of the spread will
· be less piquant.

Fish salad *(Sałatka z dorsza wędzonego)*

6 Servings

1½ lb. smoked cod or   4 tablespoons olive oil
   haddock   juice 1–2 lemons
2 large onions   lettuce leaves

Boil fish in unsalted water for 10 to 15 minutes. Strain and remove bones and skin. Flake fish. Peel onions and chop very finely. Put fish and onions into a deep dish. Mix oil and lemon juice and marinade fish in this for a few hours.
  Serve on washed, dried lettuce leaves.

Fish dishes are very popular in Poland. The Baltic provides all sorts of fish including cod, herrings and plaice. Freshwater fish are also much liked and salmon, carp, pike and trout are considered delicacies.

Most Polish housewives prefer to buy fish alive as they can then be sure of its freshness — I well remember many small country inns where the trout was caught while the guests were waiting.

As in other predominantly Catholic countries, fish is eaten on Fridays and Fast days, of which there are many, and there is a great variety of dishes — Polish fish cake, for example, is much more exciting than the English kind!

Fried fish *(Ryba smażona)*

6 Servings

2½ lb. fillet of fish
2 teaspoons salt
½ teaspoon pepper
1 tablespoon sugar
1 onion
2 oz. flour

2 eggs
2 tablespoons water
4 oz. dried breadcrumbs
4 oz. butter
lemon and parsley

Rub fish with salt, pepper and sugar. Sprinkle with chopped onion and let it stand for at least 2 hours, but preferably overnight, in a cold place. Discard onion. Dip fillets in flour. Beat eggs with water and dip fish in this and then in breadcrumbs. Fry in butter till golden. Put in a roasting tin and bake in moderate oven (375° F. or Gas mark 4) for 20 minutes. Garnish with slices of lemon and sprigs of parsley.

Pike in batter *(Szczupak w cieście)*

4 Servings

4 fillets of pike
or cod

salt
pinch pepper

Batter:

4 oz. flour
¼ pint milk

1 egg
pinch salt

Frying:

3 oz. butter or oil

Rub fish with salt and pepper and allow to stand for 1 hour. Sieve flour and add milk, egg and salt, stirring well. The batter should be fairly thick. Dip pieces of fish in batter and fry in hot fat on both sides until golden. Drain on kitchen or tissue paper. Serve hot with sauce tartare (see page 122).

Fried eel *(Węgorz smażony)*

6 Servings

2 lb. eel	4 peppercorns
1½ teaspoons salt	1 bay leaf
1 pint water	¼ teaspoon pepper
1 small onion	2 eggs
1 carrot	3 oz. dried breadcrumbs
sprig parsley	4 oz. butter

Cut skin around head. Turn it back and pull off to tail end. Hold eel over flame to burst second skin which also has to be removed. Now wash fish, cut into thick rounds and sprinkle with salt. Let it stand until stock is boiling. This stock consists of the water, chopped onion, scraped carrot, parsley, seasoning with peppercorns and the rest of the salt. Put eel into the stock and simmer for 5 minutes. (Keep stock to make soup.) Remove fish and dry well with teacloth or napkin. Beat eggs with fork on a plate. Put breadcrumbs on another plate and dip each piece first into egg and then into breadcrumbs. Fry in hot butter till golden. Serve with caper sauce (see page 115).

Fish in egg and breadcrumbs *(Ryba panierowana)*

4 Servings

4 fillets of cod	3 oz. fat for frying
½ teaspoon salt	parsley, lemon slice,
2 oz. flour	horseradish
2 eggs	
3 oz. dried breadcrumbs	

Wash fish and salt it. Dip in flour, in beaten eggs and lastly in breadcrumbs. Fry until golden on both sides. Put into moderate oven (375°F. or Gas mark 4) for 15 minutes. Put one next to other on flat dish and decorate with sprigs of parsley, slices of lemon and grated horseradish. Serve with potatoes and a salad.

Fish cake *(Tort z ryby)*

6 Servings

2 lb. cod	4 eggs
1 teaspoon sugar	$\frac{1}{4}$ teaspoon pepper
1$\frac{1}{2}$ teaspoons salt	juice of $\frac{1}{2}$ lemon
3 oz. butter	2 tablespoons thick
2 medium-sized onions	cream
3 oz. dried breadcrumbs	butter and breadcrumbs
few sprigs parsley	for cake tin

Wash fish and put in china or earthenware dish. Sprinkle with sugar and $\frac{1}{2}$ teaspoon salt and stand for 1 hour. Melt butter, peel and chop onions and add with fish to butter. Stew gently for 15 minutes. Remove bones from fish and put it twice through the mincer together with onions, breadcrumbs and parsley. Add yolks, pepper, lemon juice and cream and mix thoroughly. Fold in stiffly beaten whites. Grease and breadcrumb a 10-inch cake tin and fill with the mixture. Bake in a moderate oven (375° F. or Gas mark 4) for 1 hour.

If eaten hot, serve with lemon or caper sauce (see page 115). It is equally good cold served with sauce tartare (see page 122).

Pike in mayonnaise *(Szczupak w majonezie)*

8–10 Servings

3 lb. pike	2 pieces celery
2 teaspoons salt	6 peppercorns
2 large onions	2 bay leaves
2 carrots	water

Decoration:

lemon slices	1 egg, hard-boiled
	sweet pickles

Clean and salt pike. Make stock with all the other ingredients, allowing enough water to cover the fish. When simmered for 45 minutes, remove from heat, allow to cool and strain. Now fillet the fish, put it into the stock and simmer for 30 minutes, when it should be tender. Allow to cool. Carefully take out pieces and put them together on dish as if fish were whole again. Cover with mayonnaise (see page 118) and put into a cold place. When the mayonnaise is set, decorate with slices of egg, lemon and pickles.

Carp in Polish sauce *(Karp w szarym sosie)*

6 Servings

3 lb. carp	2 oz. honeycake*
2 teaspoons salt	1 oz. sultanas
1 onion	1 oz. almonds, chopped
1 carrot	1 teaspoon vinegar
1½ pints water	1 teaspoon sugar
2 oz. flour	
4 oz. butter	

* *Honeycake can be bought in Continental food stores or food departments of large stores.*

Ask your fishmonger to cut carp in cutlets. Wash and sprinkle with 1 teaspoon salt. Allow it to lie for 30 minutes while you prepare the stock. Peel onion, scrape carrot and put them and the rest of the salt into the boiling water. Simmer for 30 minutes. Strain and keep the liquid. Put fish into this and simmer, uncovered, for 20 minutes. Take out carefully with a fish slice and keep hot on a plate over hot water. Mix flour with melted butter and gradually add ½ pint of the fish stock, stirring all the time. Add grated honeycake and the rest of the ingredients. Simmer for 10 minutes. Pour hot sauce over the fish on the serving dish. Serve with little dumplings (page 29) or potatoes.

Salmon in aspic *(Łosoś w galarecie)*

6 Servings

2 lb. salmon	2 pints water
1½ teaspoons salt	2 egg whites
1 small onion	1 oz. gelatine
1 carrot	juice of 1 lemon
small piece parsley	4 oz. cooked peas
or celeriac root	1 egg, hard-boiled

Prepare this dish a day in advance. Have the salmon cut into 6 slices and put them into a china or earthenware bowl. Sprinkle with salt and allow to stand for 1 hour. Put the rest of the salt, onion, carrot and celeriac root into cold water. Bring to the boil and simmer until the vegetables are soft (about 30 minutes). Strain. Put fish into saucepan, pour hot stock over it and simmer for 15 minutes. Take fish out carefully and remove skin and bones. Add egg whites and gelatine to stock and allow this to dissolve. Strain through muslin. The whites will clarify of the stock.

Put the fish into a deep dish and decorate with slices of carrot, egg and peas. When the aspic begins to set but is still liquid, pour carefully over fish and put it into a cold place.

Salmon à la Polonaise *(Łosoś po polsku)*

6 Servings

2 lb. salmon	¼ pint dry white wine
3 oz. bacon, sliced	1½ oz. butter
1 teaspoon salt	1 tablespoon flour
juice of 1 lemon	

Buy salmon in one piece. Cut one slice of bacon into narrow strips and, using a larding needle, thread slices of bacon through the top of the fish. Rub the fish with

54

salt, wrap the rest of bacon around the salmon and secure it with thread. Put into a hot oven (425° F. or Gas mark 6) in a fireproof dish or roasting tin and roast for 15 minutes. Baste with lemon juice and wine and allow another 10 minutes. Cream butter with flour, add liquid from the roasting tin and bring to the boil. Simmer for 5 minutes and pour over fish before serving.

Stuffed pike *(Szczupak „po żydowsku")*

6 Servings

3–3½ lb. pike with head	2 teaspoons salt
4 oz. fresh breadcrumbs	pinch pepper
2 large onions	1 teaspoon sugar
2 egg yolks	chopped parsley
	water or fish stock

If the scales have not been removed by fishmonger, scrape them off. Remove the lower jaw and innards. Cut through the spine next to the head so that you can peel off the skin without tearing it. Roll it back to the tail, leave this on skin and remove flesh and bones. Mince meat twice or chop finely. Add breadcrumbs, grated onions, and all the other ingredients to flesh and mix well. Turn back skin and stuff loosely. Sew up the opening. Simmer slowly in fish kettle in water or preferably in stock for 1 hour. Put the fish on a long dish and cut into slices with a sharp knife.

Serve with vegetables around it, vinegar, oil and mustard sauce (see page 120). This dish is usually eaten cold.

Carp in jelly *(Karp w galarecie)*

6–8 Servings

3½–4 lb. carp with head	2 bay leaves
3 teaspoons salt	7 peppercorns
2 teaspoons sugar	juice 1–2 lemons
3 pints water	1 oz. blanched almonds
3 onions	carrots and
2 carrots	2 hard-boiled eggs
1 stick celery	for decoration

Ask your fishmonger to cut fish in even slices and to remove the gall bladder or fish will be bitter. Wash fish, sprinkle with salt and sugar and let it stand for 2 hours. In a large saucepan (pieces of fish must lie next to each other, not on top of one another) bring water with vegetables and seasonings to boil. Put in fish and let it simmer, uncovered, until tender (about 20 minutes). Carefully remove pieces and leave only the head with vegetables to simmer for another 40 minutes. By then the water should be greatly reduced and the gelatine, contained in the head, released to make it jelly. Put a little of the liquid, after having added lemon juice to the whole, into a deep dish and allow it to set in a cold place. Decorate with split almonds, carrots cut out with a small cutter and, if wanted, slices of hard-boiled egg. Put pieces of fish on this and pour over more of the liquid. Leave it to set for use the next day. If there is more liquid than the dish can take, serve it separately in a sauce boat.

Pickled trout *(Pstrąg marynowany)*

6–8 Servings

3 lb. trout
2 teaspoons salt
1 onion
1 carrot
piece parsley root

1 bay leaf
6 peppercorns
1½ pints water
1 teaspoon sugar
2 tablespoons vinegar
(preferably Tarragon)
¼ pint white wine

Clean trout and cut whole fish into pieces. Sprinkle with 1 teaspoon salt. Peel the onion, scrape the carrot, and with the parsley root, bay leaf and peppercorns bring to the boil in the water. Simmer for 15 minutes. Add the other ingredients and the fish and simmer until the fish is tender (about 10 minutes). Remove the fish and put into deep serving dish. Chop onion and cook in stock for another 15 minutes. Allow the liquid to cool and strain. Pour over the fish and let it stand in a cold place for 2 days before serving it. Use as an hors-d'oeuvre or as a main dish.

Pike or carp in wine *(Szczupak lub karp w winie)*

6 Servings

2½ lb. fish with head
2½ oz. butter
1 large onion
2 teaspoons salt

5 peppercorns
1 bay leaf
¼ pint white wine
parsley sprigs

Clean and wash fish and cut into thick cutlets. Melt butter, peel and chop onion and fry till golden. Put the fish, including the head, into the same saucepan and add all other ingredients. Cover and cook slowly for 30 minutes. Serve fish on a long plate, put together in its original shape with head. Remove the peppercorns and bay leaf and pour liquid over it. Surround with boiled or fried potatoes and decorate with sprigs of parsley.

Baked perch with mushrooms *(Sandacz zapiekany z pieczarkami)*

4 Servings

2 lb. perch	1 teaspoon pepper
8 oz. mushrooms	small carton thin cream
4 oz. butter	2 oz. grated cheese
1 large onion	2 oz. butter
2 teaspoons salt	4 tablespoons
	breadcrumbs

Ask the fishmonger to slice fish into cutlets. Wash fish and mushrooms. Put cutlets into fireproof dish and pour melted butter over it. Put into a moderate oven (375° F. — Gas Mark 4) for 10–12 minutes. Chop mushrooms finely. Peel onion and slice thinly into rings. Add mushrooms and onions with 1–2 tablespoons of water to fish. Cook another 10 minutes. Add salt and pepper to cream, pour over fish and sprinkle cheese over. Have ready breadcrumbs fried in butter and also sprinkle over the dish. Cook for futher 10 minutes before serving.

Meat and poultry

The Poles like meat, though in the
country the farmer will only have it
when he kills one of his livestock.
Then none of it is wasted, sausages
are made, the offal used in various
ways, and often friends are invited
to a special party.

Meat is frequently served with
gravy, enriched by sour cream. Gravy
powder is unknown in Poland and if a
thickening is required, flour alone is
used. The most important thing for
a good gravy is to scrape off the
residue at the sides of the roasting
tin, as this has the best flavour. If
vegetables are cooked together with
the meat, they are passed through
a sieve, which also makes a thick
gravy. Onions are used freqently and
they, too, sieved after they are soft
and the meat is ready, enrich and
flavour the gravy.

Beef à la Hussar *(Pieczeń husarska)*

This roast is named after a famous Polish cavalry regiment with a long and glorious history.

6 Servings

¼ pint vinegar	2 tablespoons flour
¾ pint stock or water	3 oz. butter
3 lb. sirloin	1 large onion
salt	¼ pint red wine
pepper	

Stuffing:

2 oz. fresh breadcrumbs	salt
1 oz. butter	pepper
1 onion	1 egg

Bring vinegar and stock to the boil and pour over meat. Strain and keep liquid. Rub meat with salt and pepper, dip in flour on all sides and quickly brown in butter. Cut onion into large slices and add this to the meat with the wine and stock, and braise for 2 hours.

Meanwhile prepare the stuffing: fry the breadcrumbs in butter, then mix with grated onion and seasoning, and finally the beaten egg. Take out the meat and put on meat board. Cut into thin slices but alternate slices should not be cut through so that you have 2 slices together. Put stuffing between these and secure either with a skewer or thread to keep stuffing in place. Add wine to gravy, return meat to pan and simmer slowly for 30 minutes.

Polish beef rolls *(Zrazy polskie zawijane)*

4 Servings

4 slices steak (about	3 oz. butter
6 oz. meat per person)	2 oz. dried breadcrumbs
1 teaspoon salt	1 tablespoon flour
1 teaspoon pepper	$\frac{1}{2}$ pint stock or water
1 large onion	2 tablespoons tomato
	purée

Ask your butcher to beat the steaks very thinly. If you like, cut them in half so that there are 2 rolls per person. Sprinkle meat with salt and pepper. Peel onion and bake until soft (this can be done the previous day if you happen to use the oven) and grate or mash it. Melt the butter in the saucepan in which the rolls are going to be cooked. Take a tablespoon of butter and add this and breadcrumbs to onion. Mix and put some of this on each roll. Tie up each roll. Coat with flour and brown in butter. The rolls must lie next to each other, i.e. the saucepan should be just large enough to fit them in. Add stock, tomatoe purée and simmer, covered, for 20 minutes longer. Serve with kasza (see page 118).

Beef olives *(Zraziki)*

6 Servings

12 thin slices of beef
(about 2 lb.)
1½ teaspoons salt
½ teaspoon pepper
8 oz. buckwheat, cooked
(see kasza, page 108)

4 slices streaky bacon
1 large onion
2 oz. flour
4 oz. butter
½ pint water

Ask your butcher to beat the meat for you. Rub each piece with salt and pepper. Put the cooked buckwheat into a basin. Chop up bacon and onion and fry together. Add this to buckwheat and put a little of this stuffing on each slice of meat. Roll up and either secure with skewers or tie thread round each roll. Dip each into flour and quickly brown in butter. Put into saucepan and add water. Simmer slowly for 1½ hours. Serve with vegetables.

Boiled brisket of beef *(Sztuka mięsa)*

6 Servings

4 lb. brisket of beef
(preferably on the bone)
1 large or 2 small
onions
2 carrots

1 stick celery
3 bay leaves
1 teaspoon marjoram
6 peppercorns
1 teaspoon salt
3 pints water

Put meat into large saucepan. Peel and chop onion, carrots and celery and add all the other ingredients. Cover meat with water and put a wellfitting lid on the saucepan. Bring to the boil and reduce heat so that the liquid simmers. Cook for 3 hours or until the meat is tender. Take it out and serve hot with horseradish sauce (see page 117). Strain stock and serve separately as soup with vermicelli, liver dumplings or other additions to soup (see page 29).

Beef pot roast *(Sztufada)*

6 Servings

4 oz. fat bacon	3 tomatoes
3 lb. sirloin or roasting	2 onions
beef	3 carrots
2 teaspoons salt	6 peppercorns
1 teaspoon pepper	2 bay leaves
3 oz. butter	½ pint water

Cut bacon into narrow strips and lard meat with it. Rub with salt and pepper and quickly brown on all sides in butter. Chop up vegetables and add these and the seasoning to the meat. Add boiling water, cover saucepan tightly and simmer very slowly for 3 hours. Make gravy by passing liquid and vegetables through a sieve. Serve with macaroni, potatoes or rice and vegetables.

Layer pie *(Zapiekana potrawa z mięsem)*

4 Servings

1½ lb. potatoes	horseradish sauce
2 eggs	(see page 117)
12 oz. cold brisket of beef★	
salt	

★ *Any cooked meat left over from a previous meal can be substituted*

Boil potatoes in their skins. Peel while hot and slice. Grease a fireproof dish and line with potatoes. Hardboil eggs, peel and slice. Put a layer of egg on the potatoes, season, then add layer of thinly sliced meat. Repeat until all ingredients are used, ending with potatoes. Pour horseradish sauce over the whole and bake in a moderately hot oven (400° F. or Gas mark 5).

Braised steak à la Nelson *(Zrazy nelsońskie)*

4 Servings

1½ lb. frying steak	8 oz. onions
2 oz. fat	½ pint water
1 teaspoon salt	1 carton sour cream
pinch pepper	or yoghourt

Beat the meat to ¼-inch thickness or ask the butcher to do it for you. Melt fat and quickly fry the steaks on both sides. Remove from frying pan, then salt and pepper, the meat lightly rubbing it in. Chop the onions very finely and fry slowly in fat left from frying the meat. Using a heavy saucepan put in the meat, alternating with onions, until all are used up. Add boiling water and slowly simmer the meat in the tightly covered saucepan. After 1 hour add sour cream and heat through, but do not allow to simmer any more. Serve with boiled potatoes.

Variation: Add 4 oz. thinly sliced mushrooms when putting in layers of onions.

Tripe *(Flaczki)*

6 Servings

1 marrow bone	½ teaspoon pepper
1 onion	3 lb. tripe, cooked
1 stick celery	½ teaspoon ground
1 carrot	ginger
sprig parsley	pinch nutmeg
pinch marjoram	3 oz. flour
2 teaspoons salt	1 oz. butter

The best tripe is honeycomb tripe but other parts will do as well. Butchers sell tripe pre-cooked so that no special blanching and cleaning is necessary. Put all except the last 5 ingredients into a saucepan and cover with boiling water. Simmer for 1 hour. Cut tripe into narrow strips about 3 inches long and add to soup. Simmer for $2\frac{1}{2}$ hours or until the tripe is soft. Put flour into melted butter in frying pan and cook till golden. Add a little of the stock and simmer to make a thin roux. Add this to stock. Add spices and simmer for 10 minutes. Remove the marrow bone, scrape out marrow and use for dumplings (see page 29). Serve together in a casserole.

Garnish for tripe

| 1 tablespoon marjoram | 1 tablespoon sweet |
| 2 oz. grated cheese | paprika |

Put marjoram through a fine sieve (a tea strainer will do) and put it on a little plate. Serve cheese on another ano paprika on a third. Let each person help himself te these three ingredients, which should be mixed in on thd plate with the tripe. Serve deep plates for tripe. It can be eaten as a first course or as the main dish.

Ox tongue *(Ozór wołowy)*

8 Servings

1 ox tongue (pickled)   water

Wash tongue and cover with cold water. Bring to the boil, pour off water and replace. Bring to the boil again, turn the heat low and simmer, well covered, for $3-3\frac{1}{2}$ hours. When soft, take out, take off skin and gristle and serve hot, cut into slices, with horseradish relish (see page 116) or horseradish sauce (see page 117).

It can also be served hot with chopped-up hard-boiled eggs.

Ox tongue in Polish sauce *(Ozór w szarym sosie)*

8–10 *Servings*

1 ox tongue (fresh)	water
1 tablespoon salt	1 onion
	1 carrot

For sauce:

2 teaspoons sugar	1 oz. almonds, sliced
1 oz. butter	juice of 1 lemon
1½ oz. flour	lemon peel
1½ tablespoons vinegar	¼ pint white wine
2 oz. raisins or sultanas	4 lumps sugar

Wash tongue, salt it and put into boiling water (to cover) together with peeled onion and carrot. Cover and simmer for 3–3½ hours. When soft, take out. Keep the water in which it was boiled. Remove skin and gristle. Make the sauce as follows:

Melt sugar until lightly coloured. Make a roux (see page 114) and add sugar. Let it simmer for 5 minutes. Add slowly about 1 pint water in which the tongue was boiled and the vinegar. Simmer for 5 minutes. Slice the tongue and put it into a saucepan with sauce. Add all the other ingredients and simmer for 15 minutes. Serve on a flat dish, covered with sauce, and if there is some left, serve it in a sauce boat.

Roast lamb à la venison *(Pieczeń barania à la sarna)*

6–8 Servings

4 lb. leg of lamb

For marinade:

1 pint water	4 peppercorns
¼ pint vinegar	2 cloves
¼ pint red wine	3 chillies
1 onion	1 clove garlic
1 tomato	pinch each of rosemary,
2 teaspoons salt	marjoram, mace,
6 juniper berries	mustard seed, nutmeg

Mix the liquids, cut up onion and tomato and add these and all the spices and herbs to the liquid. Bring to the boil and cook for 10 minutes. Let it cool. Put meat into a deep bowl, pour marinade over it and turn the meat every day. Keep the bowl in a cool place for at least 4 days, preferably 5 or 6. Take out meat.

For roasting:

4 oz. fat bacon	pinch pepper
1 teaspoon salt	4 oz. fat or butter

Cut the bacon into thin strips and lard the meat with it. Rub with salt and pepper. Melt fat in roasting pan and roast the meat in a moderate oven (375° F. or Gas mark 4) for 2 hours, basting frequently.

For gravy

1 oz. flour	1 carton sour cream

Skim fat. Stir flour into remaining liquid and simmer for 5 minutes. Add sour cream and heat but do not allow to boil. Serve with cranberries, red cabbage (see page 94) and mashed or boiled potatoes or rice.

Lamb stew *(Ragout z baraniny)*

6–8 Servings

3 lb. lamb	2 onions
salt	1 clove garlic (see use
pinch pepper	of garlic, page 11)
2 oz. flour	3 tomatoes
4 oz. fat	½ pint stock or water
2 carrots	1 teaspoon sweet paprika
2 sticks celery	4 tablespoons red wine

Ask butcher to cut up the meat for stewing, keeping the bones as these improve the flavour. Mix salt, pepper and flour and coat the pieces of meat with this. Melt fat and quickly brown the meat on all sides. Chop up all vegetables and peel and de-seed tomatoes. Add with seasoning to meat and bones, cover with water and simmer slowly for 1½–2 hours. Dissolve paprika in wine, add and simmer for 10 minutes. Remove bones and serve with rice, buckwheat (see page 108) or potatoes.

Roast loin of pork *(Schab)*

6 Servings

4 lb. loin of pork	1 teaspoon caraway seed
2 teaspoons salt	(optional)
1 teaspoon dry	2 oz. butter
mustard	

Score fat of pork and rub meat with seasoning. Sprinkle caraway seed over it. Roast in a hot oven (425° F. or Gas mark 6) for 2½ hours, basting the cut ends frequently. Serve with apple sauce, potatoes, mashed turnips or red cabbage (see page 94).

Pickling ham *(Solenie i przyrządzanie szynki)*

Although this recipe is really only of interest to people who kill their own pigs, we thought it worth including.

The ham should be fairly thick and come from a young pig. The best size is one which weighs between 10 and 15 lb. For this weight the following proportions of pickling are chosen.

1½ lb. salt	10 cloves
1 oz. saltpetre (powdered)	2 oz. brown sugar
15 peppercorns	10 bay leaves

Dry salt on heated frying pan and mix with all the other ingredients except bay leaves. Rub mixture all over ham and around bone until it is all absorbed. Put ham into earthenware or wooden container which should be just the size to take it but not larger, as the ham should touch the sides of the container as far as possible. Put bay leaves on top of ham, cover it with a wooden board and weight this down. Leave for 24 hours in the kitchen. Then take it into a cool place (not too cold) and turn the ham every other day. Baste with the liquid which has formed. After 3 weeks the ham is ready to be used. Scrape off spices but do not wash if you want to keep it. Before cooking the ham soak it overnight in cold water.

Veal cutlets *(Zrazy wołyńskie)*

4 Servings

8 thinly cut veal cutlets	8 oz. tomatoes
	1½ teaspoons salt
8 oz. bacon	1 tablespoon flour

Wash cutlets and put into a small, heavy saucepan, a layer of cutlets alternating with bacon and sliced tomatoes. Add salt. Cover with a tight-fitting lid and simmer slowly for 1 hour. Remove meat and bacon, sprinkle flour into gravy and simmer for 7 minutes. Put meat and bacon into gravy and serve with potatoes or kasza (see page 108).

Veal goulash *(Paprykąsz cielęcy)*

4 Servings

1½ lb. stewing veal	4 large tomatoes
salt	1½ teaspoons sweet
pinch pepper	paprika
2 tablespoons flour	1 tablespoon water
4 oz. butter or fat	1 bottle plain yoghourt
3 large onions	

Cut meat into 2-inch cubes. Mix salt, pepper and flour and roll meat in this mixture. Melt 2 oz. butter and fry the finely chopped onions in it till golden. Add the rest of the butter, meat and cut-up tomatoes. Simmer very slowly in a covered saucepan for 30 minutes. If the meat looks too dry, add up to ¼ pint water, otherwise continue to simmer it for another 30 minutes. Mix paprika and 1 tablespoon water and pour it into meat saucepan. Allow 15 minutes' more cooking. Add the yoghourt and heat through but do not let it boil.

Veal rolls *(Zrazy cielęce zawijane)*

4 Servings

8 thin slices of veal	salt
(about 1½ lb.)	pinch pepper

For stuffing:

1 onion	4 oz. mushrooms
1 oz. butter	2 tablespoons flour
1 tablespoon breadcrumbs	

Beat each slice of meat and rub with salt and pepper. *Make the stuffing as follows:* chop onion finely and fry till golden. Thinly slice washed but not peeled mushrooms and add these and the breadcrumbs to onion. Put a spoonful of this on each slice of meat, roll up and secure with a skewer. Dip each roll in flour. Melt butter in roasting tin, put rolls into it and cook in a moderate oven (375° F. or Gas mark 4) for 45 minutes. Serve with rice.

Stuffed breast of veal *(Mostek cielęcy, nadziewany)*

6 Servings

4 lb. breast of veal	3 oz. butter
salt	pepper

For stuffing:

4 bread rolls	chopped parsley
¼ pint milk	1 onion
salt	1 oz. butter
pinch pepper	1 egg
pinch marjoram	

Ask your butcher to cut a pocket in the veal for the stuffing. Rub meat with salt and pepper. Soak rolls in milk for 20 minutes and squeeze out liquid. Add egg, salt, pepper, marjoram and parsley. Chop onion finely and fry in butter. Put all together and mix well. Fill pocket and close with skewer or sew up. Melt butter and roast meat, covered, for 2 hours in a moderate oven (375° F. or Gas mark 4) and then uncover and allow another 20 minutes. Serve with salad or vegetables.

Leg of venison *(Sarnina z bajcu)*

10–12 Servings

8 oz. butter	½ pint thick cream
6 lb. leg of venison	1 lemon
3 teaspoons salt	3 oz. flour
3 tablespoons brandy	

For marinade:

1 bottle red wine	3 cloves garlic
½ pint oil	2 bay leaves
½ pint vinegar	6 peppercorns
1 large sliced onion	4 cloves
2 carrots	1½ pints water

Wash meat. Prepare marinade by combining all the ingredients and bringing to the boil. Allow to cool and pour over meat. Leave for 3 days, turning every day, then strain marinade.

Melt butter in roasting tin. Rub meat with salt, after having dried it in a clean cloth. Brown evenly on all sides. Roast in a moderate oven (375°F. or Gas mark 4), covered, for 30 minutes. Add part of strained marinade, cover again and roast for 1 hour. Baste frequently and add more marinade. Roast for another hour, pour brandy over meat and uncover. Make a golden roux (see page 114), add some of the cream and pour over meat. Roast for 20 minutes. Add lemon juice to the rest of the cream and add to gravy. Slice meat thinly, pour sauce over it and serve with potatoes and cranberries.

Wild boar *(Dzik)*

The wild boar is still hunted in Poland. The meat is very good, a cross between pork and venison. As it has a rather strong aroma, it is best to marinate it for 6–8 days. Here is one of the best marinades for boar:

Marinade for 10 lb. meat

3½ pints water
¾ pint vinegar
handful juniper berries
handful peppercorns
15 cloves
4 teaspoons salt

6 bay leaves
2 cloves garlic
4 onions
½ celeriac root
peel of 1 lemon

Boil all ingredients together and when cold pour over meat. Cover with a wooden dish or piece of wood, weight this down and leave in a cold place.

Saddle of boar *(Comber z dzika)*

12 Servings

6 lb. saddle
8 oz. pork belly
2 teaspoons salt
4 oz. butter

¼ pint white wine
2 tablespoons flour
1 pint soured cream

If the meat has too much fat, remove some of it. Cut pork belly in thin strips and lard meat. Rub with salt. Melt butter in roasting pan and roast boar in hot oven (425°F. or Gas mark 6) for the first 30 minutes. Lower the heat to 375°F. or Gas mark 4 and roast for 2 hours, basting it frequently. When it begins to colour, add wine and sprinkle meat with flour. Before serving, add soured cream. Cut meat thinly and serve with red cabbage or salad.

Braised boar *(Pieczeń z dzika)*

6 Servings

3 lb. meat without bone
(marinated, see
page 73)
2 teaspoons salt
3 oz. butter
2 onions
3 carrots

2 celery stalks
3 bay leaves
6 juniper berries
6 peppercorns
3 cloves
2 tablespoons tomato
purée

Beat meat and if necessary remove skin (which can be very tough). Rub with salt and put into pan with melted butter. Add vegetables and seasoning and braise. When browned on all sides, add tomato purée and wine, cover and simmer for about 2–2½ hours. During this time add several spoonfuls of strained marinade in which the meat has been lying (see page 73). When tender remove meat and put it for 20 minutes into a hot oven (425°F. or Gas mark 6) and slice thinly before serving. Pass sauce through Sieve liguid, pour some over the meat and serve the rest in a sauceboat. Serve with sharp compote (see page 121), redcurrant jelly or cranberries, and also with salads of choice.

Bigos

Bigos is one of the most famous Polish dishes. Originally it was eaten after hunting and, unlike most other cooked viands, it loses nothing through reheating but rather gains by it. Though the main ingredients are more or less the same in most recipes, no two of them are exactly alike. In his most famous book, Pan Tadeusz, the Polish poet, Adam Mickiewicz, grew lyrical when he described how bigos is served in the woods after a hunt.

'In the huge pots the bigos was cooking. One cannot express in words its flavour, its scent and its colour. Words can only be heard .... but the stomach cannot appreciate their content.

'Enclosed in the pots the cabbage's moist bosom embraces choice pieces of meat till all its living juices are extracted, and until the liquid, rising to the very edges of the pots, scents all the air around them, making it fragrant.'

In Mickiewicz's time, the famous gold-flecked wódka from Gdańsk was drunk with bigos and the toast they drank was 'Gdańsk (Danzig), once ours, will be ours once more.' This has come true, as today Gdańsk has become Polish again.

Hunters' Bigos *(Bigos myśliwski)*

6–8 Servings

1 3–4 lb. head firm white cabbage	1 lb. stewing beef knuckle of ham
2 teaspoons salt	3 tomatoes
1 lb. cooking apples	6 peppercorns
6 oz. fat (preferably lard)	$\frac{1}{2}$ teaspoon pepper
$\frac{1}{2}$ pint stock	2 teaspoons sugar
2 onions	any meat left-overs can
1 lb. fat pork	be added
8 oz. bacon in one piece	1 tablespoon flour

Wash cabbage and chop finely. Put into deep bowl and mix with salt. Cover and allow to stand for 2 hours. Squeeze out liquid. Peel and dice apples. Melt fat, add cabbage and apples and simmer, covered, for 1 hour. During this time add some of the stock. Peel and chop onions. Cut pork into small squares, put into saucepan and add onion and chopped bacon. Cover and simmer. After 20 minutes add diced beef and cook for another 20 minutes. Now add the meats to cabbage as well as

76

all other ingredients except flour. Add rest of stock and, if necessary, a little boiling water. Simmer all together for 1½ hours. Dust with flour and stir, being careful to avoid lumps. Simmer for 10 more minutes. Serve hot.

Bigos made with sauerkraut *(Bigos z kapusty kiszonej)*

6 Servings

4 oz. fat	4 oz. fat bacon in
1½ oz. sugar	1 piece
2 lb. sauerkraut	1–2 pimentos
(fresh or canned)	3 bay leaves
3 dried mushrooms,	6 peppercorns
soaked overnight	1½ pints stock or water
1 lb. fat pork	3 pairs Polish sausages
1 lb. Polish sausage in	or frankfurters
1 piece (garlic or	salt
Cracow sausage)	

Melt fat and brown sugar in it. Add sauerkraut and chopped mushrooms together with the water in which they were soaked. Simmer covered for 30 minutes, stirring frequently. Cut up pork, sausage and bacon. Add pork and bacon to sauerkraut as well as seasonings. Cook slowly for another 30 minutes. Add sausage and part of stock. (It might not be necessary to use all the stock, depending on the moisture in the sauerkraut.) After another 30 minutes add sausages, cut into 1-inch long pieces, and simmer again for 30 minutes. Taste to see if salt is needed and if so, add it now. Simmer for another 30 minutes. Serve hot in soup tureen.

This dish is even better when warmed up and can therefore be prepared on the previous day or in the morning.

Rissoles *(Klopsiki)*

6 Servings

1 lb. beef, minced	3 oz. fat
1 lb. pork, minced	2 cloves garlic
3 bread rolls	1½ teaspoons salt
¼ pint milk for soaking rolls	pinch pepper
2 onions	2 eggs
	¼ pint water

Mix meat in a deep bowl. Soak rolls for 15 minutes. Chop onions finely and fry in 1 oz. fat till golden. Chop garlic and crush it with the blade of knife together with salt on meat board. Add pepper, eggs, squeezed-out rolls, onions and garlic to meat and mix well. Melt rest of fat. Form rissoles and fry on both sides till brown. Put them into saucepan, add boiling water and cover. Simmer for 45 minutes. Serve with potatoes and green vegetables.

Stuffed peppers *(Nadziewane papryki)*

4 Servings

8 green peppers	1 teaspoon salt
12 oz. meat, minced	pinch pepper
4 tablespoons cooked rice	1 pint tomato sauce
2 grated onions	

Slit open peppers without removing top. Carefully take out *all* the pips inside as these are very hot and would spoil the dish. Mix meat, rice, onion and seasoning and stuff peppers. Tie up each pepper with thread. Prepare tomato sauce in a large saucepan. Put in peppers, cover and simmer for 1 hour. Serve with rice.

Variation: Prepare as above but cook in a casserole in a moderate oven (375° F. or Gas mark 4).

Mock hare *(Fałszywy zając)*

6 Servings

2 lb. beef, minced	1 egg
8 oz. pork, minced	2 egg yolks
5 oz. green bacon	½ carton sour cream
2 stale bread rolls	½ teaspoon pepper
¼ pint milk	2½ teaspoons salt
1 onion	4 oz. butter

Put beef and pork into a bowl. Cut bacon into strips for larding. Soak rolls in milk and when soft, squeeze out and mash with a fork. Chop onion finely. Add rolls, onion, eggs, cream and seasonings to meat and mix well. Form thick roll and lard with bacon strips to imitate hare's saddle. Melt butter in roasting tin. Put meat into hot oven (425° F. or Gas mark 6) and cover with foil. Roast for 40 minutes. Reduce heat to moderately hot (400° F. or Gas mark 5) and remove foil. Roast for another 20 minutes. Serve with cranberries.

Liver pâté *(Pasztet z wątroby)*

4 Servings

1 lb. liver	1½ teaspoons salt
2 eggs	¼ teaspoon pepper
1 onion	1 teaspoon marjoram
3 slices bread soaked	8 oz. fat bacon
in milk or water	

Mince liver. Add yolks, grated onion, bread soaked and squeezed out, seasoning and marjoram. Mix well. Fold in stiffly beaten egg whites. Line bread tin with bacon. Put mixture in and bake in moderate oven (375° F. or Gas mark 4) for 45 minutes. Before turning it out, drain off fat. Serve hot or cold.

Jellied meat *(Nóżki w galarecie)*

6 Servings

4 calves feet	2 onions
2 pig's trotters	2 celery sticks
2 teaspoons salt	6 peppercorns
2 carrots	3 bay leaves
	water

For clarifying:

2 egg whites

Blanch feet and trotters. Add all other ingredients and put into saucepan. Cover with cold water. With tight-fitting lid cover saucepan, bring to the boil, turn low and simmer for 4 hours. Remove meat from bones and cut into small squares. Cut up all vegetables and remove bay leaves and peppercorns. Strain stock and bring to the boil again. Put in whites of eggs to remove all impurities. Strain again, this time through muslin. Fill moulds with meat and vegetables and pour stock over it. Put into cold place to jelly. Serve cold with salad, oil and vinegar.

Meat balls in tomato sauce *(Bitki w sosie pomidorowym)*

6 Servings

2 lb. meat, minced	1½ teaspoons salt
4 slices bread	½ teaspoon pepper
water or milk for soaking bread	2 eggs
2 large onions	2 tablespoons flour
2 cloves garlic	tomato sauce

Put meat in bowl. Soak bread for 10 minutes and squeeze out. Grate onions. Chop garlic on meat board and add salt, crushing these together with the flat blade of a knife. Add everything except flour and sauce to meat. Form into small balls and sprinkle with flour. Simmer in tomato sauce for 1 hour. Serve with boiled potatoes.

Lithuanian ravioli *(Kołduny litewskie)*

4 Servings

ravioli (page 42)

For filling:

6 oz. lean lamb without bone	1 clove garlic
6 oz. steak	½ teaspoon salt
4 oz. suet	¼ teaspoon pepper
1 small onion	good pinch marjoram
	1 tablespoon water

Remove all skin or fat from meats and mince or chop finely with suet. Peel onion and grate. Crush garlic with salt (see page 11) and add this and all other ingredients to meat. Thinly roll out dough and cut into rounds with wine glass or cutter. Fill well in centre, fold over edges which were dampened with moist finger or pastry brush. Continue as for ravioli (see page 42). Serve in soup plates with clear soup.

Variation:

For topping:

2 oz. butter	4 tablespoons dried breadcrumbs

Prepare and cook as before but instead of serving with soup, served covered with fried breadcrumbs.

Meat loaf *(Pieczeń siekana)*

6 Servings

1 lb. minced beef	2 teaspoons salt
1 lb. minced pork	½ teaspoon pepper
8 oz. minced veal	2 eggs
2 large onions	4 oz. fresh breadcrumbs
2 oz. butter	2 oz. fat for roasting
1 clove garlic (see use of garlic, page 11)	

For gravy:

1 oz. flour	¼ pint thin cream
2 tablespoons water	

Mix the meats in a deep bowl. Chop onions finely and fry till golden. Add this and all the other ingredients except fat to meats. Melt fat in roasting tin. Form 2 loaves with the mixture, put them into tin and cook in a moderate oven (375°F. or Gas mark 4) for 1 hour, basting frequently. To make gravy remove meat and scrape off the residue at the bottom and sides of roasting tin as this will give the gravy its flavour. Sprinkle flour into tin, mix with residue, add water and let cook for 5 minutes. Add cream and allow another minute or two. Serve gravy separately with the hot meat.

This loaf is also very good eaten cold.

Stuffed meat loaf *(Pieczeń nadziewana)*

6 Servings

meat loaf (see previous recipe)

For stuffing:

8 oz. buckwheat (see kasza, page 108)	4 oz. streaky bacon

Prepare loaf as in previous recipe but before putting it into roasting tin have stuffing ready by mixing cooked buckwheat with chopped bacon. Divide meat in half to make 2 loaves. Put each half between 2 sheets of greaseproof paper and roll out fairly thinly. Remove top paper and spread half of the stuffing on meat. Roll up like a Swiss roll. When both loaves are stuffed, put them into roasting tin side by side and continue as for previous recipe.

Chicken liver pâté *(Pasztet z wątróbki z kury)*

6 Servings

1 lb. chicken livers	4 eggs
1 large onion	1½ teaspoons salt
1 oz. fat	¼ teaspoon ginger
4–5 slices bread soaked	pinch nutmeg
in milk	butter and breadcrumbs
2 cloves garlic	for pudding basin
4 oz. butter	

Wash the livers and remove skins. Peel onion, chop finely and fry in fat but do not let it get coloured. Add livers and simmer for about 10 minutes. After this time the livers should not be red any more, nor should they be allowed to get brown. Squeeze out bread and add to onion and liver mixture. Peel garlic, chop and crush with a little salt (see page 11) and add to mixture. Cream butter, add egg yolks, and seasoning. Whisk whites until stiff. Mince liver mixture twice or pass through sieve. Add all the other ingredients, fold in egg whites. Grease and breadcrumb the pudding basin, fill three-quarters of it with mixture, cover and steam in saucepan for 1 hour. Serve hot or cold.

Variation: The pâté can also be baked in a fireproof dish in a moderate oven (375° F. or Gas mark 4) for 40 minutes.

Chicken the Polish way *(Kurczęta pieczone po polsku)*

4 Servings

2 small young chickens	4 oz. butter
1½ teaspoons salt	8 oz. fresh
fresh dill	breadcrumbs
1 tablespoon fresh	
parsley	

For roasting:

2 oz. butter

Wash chickens, salt inside and outside. Chop dill and parsley finely. Melt butter and put in breadcrumbs. Allow butter to be absorbed by crumbs, but do not fry to colour. Add dill, parsley and rest of salt to this and stuff chickens with the mixture.

Melt butter in roasting tin and put chickens in moderately hot oven (400°F. or Gas mark 5) for 45 minutes–1 hour. Baste frequently and serve hot, with vegetables and rice or potatoes or kasza see page 108.

Chicken with gooseberry sauce *(Potrawa z kury z agrestem)*

4–6 Servings

1 large boiling chicken	1½ lb. fresh gooseberries
1 onion	1 dessertspoon sugar
1 carrot	1 oz. butter
2 bay leaves	1½ oz. flour
6 peppercorns	4 tablespoons sour
2 teaspoons salt	cream
water	

Wash chicken inside and out. Dice onion and carrot for stock and put this with bay leaves, peppercorns and

salt into pot. Add chicken and cover with water. Bring
to boil and simmer until soft. Remove chicken, strain
stock and in it, simmer the washed, topped and tailed,
gooseberries and sugar for 15 minutes. Strain stock
again, reserving gooseberries. Make a white roux (see
page 114) and add stock to make 1 pint stirring all the
time. Add gooseberries. Remove skin from chicken and
cut into neat joints. Pour gooseberry sauce over it and
slowly cook for 15 minutes. Just before serving add sour
cream. Serve in a deep dish.

Excellent chicken rissoles *(Wyborne bitki z kury)*

4 Servings

2 chicken breasts	2 oz. truffles or
½ oz. butter	mushrooms (canned)
2 eggs	½ teaspoon salt
2 slices bread soaked	pinch pepper
in milk	

For frying:

egg and breadcrumbs   2 oz. butter

Remove skin from chicken breasts. Mince twice. Separate
eggs. Cream butter and egg yolks, add bread, squeezed
out and mashed, minced chicken, seasoning and the
stiffly beaten egg whites. Chop truffles or mushrooms.
Form mixture into balls the size of a plum and put
a little of the chopped mushroom in the centre of each.
Roll in egg and breadcrumbs and fry in butter until
golden all round. Put for 5–8 minutes into hot oven
(425° F. or Gas mark 6) to make sure that rissoles are
cooked through inside. Serve with a sharp sauce (see
page 121).

Chicken risotto *(Risotto z kury)*

4–5 Servings

1 boiling chicken	8 oz. rice
2 teaspoons salt	6 oz. grated cheese
1 onion	1 oz. butter
6 peppercorns	2 tablespoons tomato
1 clove garlic	purée
2 bay leaves	
water	

Wash and joint chicken and place in a saucepan with salt, chopped onion, peppercorns, crushed garlic (see page 11) and bay leaves. Cover with cold water, bring to the boil, skim off impurities and simmer, covered, until tender (about 2 hours, depending on the age of the chicken). Remove the chicken and strain stock. Wash rice in several waters, place in saucepan with butter and tomato purée, and just cover with stock, keeping aside any surplus. Simmer for 10 minutes. Grease a fireproof dish and put in alternate layers of chicken and rice, which has been mixed with cheese. End with rice and pour $\frac{1}{4}$ pint of the stock over it. Put into hot oven (425–450°F. or Gas mark 6–7) and let it cook for 25–30 minutes.

Roast stuffed duck *(Kaczka nadziewana)*

4 Servings

1 (2$\frac{1}{2}$–3 lb.) duck	2 teaspoons marjoram
2$\frac{1}{2}$ teaspoons salt	1$\frac{1}{2}$ oz. butter

Stuffing:

4 slices bread	1 small onion
$\frac{1}{4}$ pint milk	1 oz. butter
dash pepper	duck liver
1 teaspoon marjoram	1 egg

Wash duck inside and outside. An hour before putting it into the oven, rub both inside and outside with salt and marjoram. Now prepare stuffing: soak bread in milk. When soft, squeeze out and add pepper and marjoram. Peel onion and chop finely. Fry in butter until transparent, then add liver. Cook quickly for 2–3 minutes, turning liver. When no more blood is to be seen, remove pan from heat and chop the liver. Add chopped onion and liver, egg yolk and stiffly beaten egg white to the bread mixture and stuff duck with it. Melt butter in roasting tin, then place the duck in it. Put into a hot oven (425–450°F. or Gas mark 6–7) for 15 minutes, then decrease heat to 400°F. or Gas mark 5 and allow 1¼ hours for roasting, basting frequently. If the roasting tin becomes too dry, add a little water.

Roast goose *(Gęś pieczona)*

10–12 Servings

1 5–6 lb. goose	1–1½ lb. apples
1 tablespoon salt	4 oz. butter
1 tablespoon marjoram	

Wash goose inside and outside. Scald with boiling water. Rub inside and outside with salt and let it stand for 4 hours. Rub inside with marjoram, crushed into powder. Wash apples and core but do not peel. Stuff goose with apples. Put into a roasting tin in which half the butter has been placed. Cover goose with the rest of the butter and put either foil or greaseproof paper over the top. Roast in a hot oven (425–450°F. or Gas mark 6–7) for 1¾ hours, basting frequently. Remove paper for last 20 minutes. During the last 10 minutes sprinkle the breast three times with cold water to make the skin crisp. Take out, pour off fat and make gravy by scraping the sediment off the sides of the roasting tin and allowing it to boil for 3 minutes with natural juices. Serve with red cabbage.

Stuffed roast turkey *(Indyk pieczony nadziewany)*

15–16 Servings

1 (10–12 lb.) turkey	stuffing (see following
4 teaspoons salt	recipes)
4 oz. butter	

Wash the bird inside and outside, rub with salt and stuff. Keep giblets separately. Sew up at neck, using a strong thread and large needle. Put tail through vent and also sew up. Truss bird with skewers and string to keep it in good shape. Wrap the bird completely in foil after having put butter all over the breast and put it into a hot oven (425–450°F. or Gas mark 6–7), but reduce heat immediately to very moderate (350°F. or Gas mark 3). Allow 20 minutes' roasting per lb. turkey and 20 minutes over. Roast for two-thirds of the time, then remove foil to allow the breast to become crisp and golden. Baste frequently.

When ready, remove from oven and put on a hot dish. Remove string, thread and skewers. Serve with roast potatoes, cranberry sauce, sprouts or salad.

Turkey stuffing with sultanas *(Farsz z rodzynkami)*

turkey liver	pinch nutmeg
3 eggs	pinch ground cloves
1½ oz. butter	1 teaspoon sugar
2 tablespoons dried	2 tablespoons chopped
breadcrumbs	parsley
½ teaspoon salt	4 oz. sultanas
pinch pepper	

Chop liver very finely. Cream egg yolks with butter and add to liver together with all the seasonings and washed and dried sultanas. Lastly beat egg whites stiffly and fold in. Stuff turkey with mixture.

Variation:

turkey liver	pinch nutmeg
8 oz. liver	pinch ginger
2 tablespoons dried	4 oz. pork fat or bacon
breadcrumbs	3 eggs
½ teaspoon salt	1 oz. butter
pinch pepper	

Mince livers and cut pork fat in very small squares. Mix together all ingredients except eggs and butter. Cream egg yolks and butter and incorporate into mixture. Fold in stiffly beaten egg whites and stuff turkey with mixture.

Turkey stuffing with chestnuts *(Nadzianie z kasztanami*

1 lb. fresh chestnuts   1½ oz. butter

Boil chestnuts until they are almost soft, then cook in 1½ oz. butter until completely soft. The chestnuts should remain whole. Stuff turkey with these.

Creamed chestnut stuffing for turkey
(Farsz słodki z kasztanów)

1 lb. fresh chestnuts	4 tablespoons thick
1 oz. butter	cream
3 eggs	1 teaspoon sugar
3 tablespoons dried	
breadcrumbs	

Boil chestnuts until soft (see page 10). Mince twice or pass through sieve. Cream butter with egg yolks until foamy, add breadcrumbs, cream and sugar. Whisk egg whites till very stiff and fold in, alternating with chestnuts. Stuff the neck end of the turkey with this.

Turkey stuffing with meat and chestnuts *(Farsz z mięsa kasztanów)*

8 oz. fat pork
4 oz. stewing veal
4 oz. fat belly of pork
or bacon
2 slices bread soaked
in milk
1 egg

pinch pepper
pinch nutmeg
½ teaspoon salt
2 onions
1½ oz. butter
8 oz. chestnuts

Boil chestnuts (see page 10). (The chestnuts should be left whole.) Put the meats twice through mincer. Squeeze out bread and add with egg and seasoning. Peel onions, chop and fry in butter. Add onions and the boiled chestnuts to this mixture and stuff turkey with it.

Vegetables

A country which is snowbound in the winter, and for economic reasons has to be self-sufficient, has to use home-grown vegetables which will keep well. This accounts for the great variety of cabbage dishes as cabbage is easily stored. Onions and garlic too keep well and are widely used, as are herbs, of which dill is the most popular. During the winter this can only be used dried, but when fresh it makes an excellent sauce of delicate flavour. The thin, green fronds, chopped finely and sprinkled over new potatoes, turn these into a dish fit for kings. Dill is easily grown and deserves recognition where it has not yet found it.

Vegetables à la polonaise, as they are called in culinary language, are covered with breadcrumbs fried golden in butter. This turns a humble cauliflower into a more interesting dish. The method can be applied to other boiled vegetables such as beans and brussel sprouts. Cabbage and many other vegetables are not boiled but cut small and put into hot fat to which, after a short time, a little boiling water is added, enough to soften the vegetable and to be absorbed by it. This method preserves vitamins which are otherwise lost. It also improves the flavour.

Runner beans *(Fasola na kwaśno)*

4 Servings

1½ lb. runner beans	1 oz. butter
½ teaspoon salt	1 oz. flour
1 pint water	
1½ tablespoons vinegar	

If beans are old pare off string on each side and slice into ¼ inch thick pieces, cutting at an angle. Young beans can be cooked whole after the stalks have been removed.

Wash beans and put into boiling, salted water, cover and simmer until soft. (This depends on the age of beans but can be as much as 30 minutes.) Strain but keep the water.

Put the beans into an empty saucepan, add butter, sprinkle flour over it and add vinegar. Bring to the boil, stir to avoid lumps and add a little of the water in which the beans have been boiled. Allow to cook for 5 minutes.

Beetroot *(Buraki)*

4 Servings

5 medium-sized beetroot, cooked	1 tablespoon vinegar salt
1½ oz. butter	¼ pint soured cream
1 oz. flour	

Peel beetroot and grate. Make a roux (see page 114) with butter and flour, and add vinegar, salt and beetroot to this. Cook for 3–5 minutes. Add soured cream and heat but do not boil any more.

Variation: Use ¼ pint milk and 2 tablespoons lemon juice instead of cream.

Cabbage *(Kapusta)*

6 Servings

1 cabbage (about 2 lb.)	1½ oz. butter
1 teaspoon salt	1 oz. flour
water	

Divide cabbage in half and cut out a V-shaped piece in the centre of the stalk. Leave in salted water for 10 minutes to remove insects. Rinse. Put into boiling, salted water, cover and simmer for 15 minutes. Strain and keep about ½ pint of water. Make a roux (see page 114) of butter and flour. Chop cabbage and add to the roux, add a little of the water (you might not need it all), cover and simmer for about 20 minutes or until the cabbage is soft.

Variation: Add crushed clove of garlic and ½ teaspoon caraway seed when putting cabbage into roux.

Cabbage with apples *(Kapusta z jabłkami)*

4 Servings

1½ lb. cabbage
2 large cooking
apples
2 fat bacon rashers
1 onion

1 tablespoon flour
1 teaspoon sugar
salt
⅛ pint boiling water

Remove coarse or faded outside leaves and chop cabbage. Scald with boiling water. Peel apples and chop. Slice onion very thinly and fry together with chopped bacon. Put cabbage, apples and bacon into saucepan, add sugar and salt and boiling water. Cover and simmer for 30 minutes. Sprinkle with flour, stirring well to avoid lumps. Cook for another 10 minutes.

Variation: Add 8 oz. tomatoes, washed and sliced, at the time when adding cabbage to bacon.

Red cabbage *(Czerwona kapusta)*

4 Servings

2 lb. red cabbage
1 tablespoon salt
¼ pint red wine
1 oz. butter
1 oz. flour

2 teaspoons sugar
pinch pepper
pinch ground cloves
pinch cinnamon

Shred cabbage finely and sprinkle with salt. Let stand for 15 minutes then drain. Cover with boiling water (but only cover, so that no water stands above the cabbage) and simmer slowly until soft but not mushy. Make a roux of butter and flour (see page 114), cream it with a little of the cabbage liquid and add to the cabbage together with all the other ingredients. Cook for 5 more minutes.

Red cabbage with chestnuts *(Czerwona kapusta z kasztanami)*

6 Servings

2 lb. cabbage	¾ pint stock
8 oz. dried chestnuts	2 tablespoons vinegar
soaked overnight	1½ teaspoons salt
(see page 10)*	1 teaspoon sugar
1 onion	2 tablespoons flour
2 oz. fat	

* *dried chestnuts are obtainable at many continental shops. If fresh chestnuts are used, double the quantity and prepare as described on page 10.*

Shred cabbage finely. Boil chestnuts for 45 minutes. Discard water. Chop onion finely and cook in fat until golden. Add cabbage, stock and other ingredients except flour and simmer, covered, for 30 minutes. Add chestnuts and simmer for another 30 minutes. For the last 10 minutes sprinkle with flour, stirring well to avoid lumps.

Cauliflower *(Kalafior)*

4 Servings

1 large cauliflower	2 oz. butter
1 teaspoon salt	1 oz. dried breadcrumbs
1 teaspoon sugar	

Remove leaves and soak cauliflower in cold salt water for 15 minutes to remove insects. Rinse. Have boiling, salted water ready, enough to cover cauliflower, add sugar and put cauliflower in, stalk end at the bottom as otherwise it might remain hard at that end. Boil for 15–20 minutes. Carefully take out cauliflower, put on a hot dish and pour over it breadcrumbs which have been fried in butter till golden.

Celeriac *(Selery)*

6 Servings

2–3 celeriac roots
2 teaspoons salt
juice 1–2 lemons
½ pint meat stock

1 oz. butter
1 oz. flour
½ teaspoon salt

Peel each celeriac (round root) and simmer in boiling, salted water until almost soft (about 40 minutes). Take out, discard water and slice fairly thinly. Pour lemon juice over it. Bring stock to boil, put celeriac with lemon juice in it, cover and allow another 15–20 minutes simmering. Make a roux (see page 114), add salt and liquid in which celeriac is cooking. Stir until smooth and add rest of liquid and celeriac. Simmer for 5 minutes. Serve with meat or fish.

Celeriac fritters *(Smażone selery)*

4 Servings

1 large celeriac root
(over 1 lb.)
2 eggs
2 oz. flour

4 oz. dried breadcrumbs
1 teaspoon salt
3 oz. fat for frying

Prepare celeriac and cook (see page 96). When almost ready, strain and cut into slices about ¼ inch thick. Whisk eggs with a fork in a deep plate. Put flour on to another plate and breadcrumbs on to a third. Dip each slice in flour, eggs and breadcrumbs to coat evenly. Have fat hot in a frying pan and fry each slice on both sides till golden. Serve with a sauce or salad.

Marrow fritters *(Oładki z kabaczków)*

4 Servings

1½ lb. marrow	½ teaspoon salt
2 oz. flour	pinch pepper
1 egg	4 oz. fat

Peel marrow and cut through. Remove seeds and grate on fine grater. Let stand for 15 minutes and squeeze out liquid. Add all ingredients except fat and mix well. Melt fat in the frying pan and put spoonfuls of mixture into the hot fat. Fry on both sides till golden. Serve hot with tomato sauce or meat.

Cucumber salad *(Mizeria)*

4–5 Servings

1 large cucumber	2 tablespoons oil
1½ teaspoons salt	½ teaspoon sweet
1 tablespoon vinegar	paprika

Peel cucumber and slice very thinly. Put into deep dish and put on salt. Let it stand, covered, for at least 1 hour. Squeeze out liquid. Mix vinegar and oil and pour over cucumber, mixing well. Sprinkle with paprika.

Variation:

1 large cucumber	pinch sugar
¼ pint thin cream	juice ½ lemon
pinch salt	fresh dill

Peel and slice cucumber as in previous recipe. Mix cream with salt, sugar and lemon juice and stir into cucumber. Sprinkle finely chopped dill over it.

Cauliflower in batter *(Kalafior w cieście)*

6 Servings

1 large cauliflower
1 teaspoon salt
1 teaspoon sugar

water to cover
cauliflower

For batter:

4 oz. self-raising flour
2 eggs
½ pint milk

½ teaspoon salt
4 oz. fat for frying

Cook cauliflower (see page 95). Strain carefully, allow to cool and divide into single pieces, breaking it into flowers as they are. Make batter (see page 50) and dip each flower into it. Have fat very hot and fry individual pieces on both sides. Serve hot with dill sauce, lemon sauce or mayonnaise (see pages 117, 118, 118).

Mixed vegetables (winter) *(Bukiet z jarzyn (zimowy)*

6 Servings

8 oz. boiled beetroot
8 oz. carrots
12 oz. brussels sprouts
1 lb. potatoes
1 or 2 pickled cucumbers
8 oz. swede
water

3½ oz. butter
1 oz. flour
1½ oz. dried breadcrumbs
salt
1 teaspoon sugar
2 teaspoons vinegar

Peel beetroots and carrots and slice very thinly or grate on coarse grater. Prepare sprouts for cooking. Peel potatoes. Peel and slice cucumbers. Scoop out small balls the size of walnuts from swede. Boil sprouts, potatoes and swede balls in separate saucepans in salted water. To swede water add also the sugar. Strain and keep hot. Melt half the butter and if carrots were grated, fry for about 5 minutes, stirring frequently. Add ¼ pint boiling, salted water and cook till soft. If sliced, cook in water straight away. Melt a little butter (about 1½ oz.) and make a roux (see page 114). Divide this and add carrots to one half and beetroots to other half. Add vinegar to the beetroots and heat through. Add 1 tablespoon water to the carrots in the roux and simmer for a few minutes. Mash potatoes. Arrange hot vegetables on large round heated dish with swede balls in centre. Cover them with fried breadcrumbs. Arrange vegetables to give the most pleasing effect by varying the colours.

Potato croquettes (Krokiety z kartofli)

4 Servings

1 lb potatoes	pinch pepper
2 eggs	4 oz. plain flour
1 teaspoon salt	8 oz. fat*

* *The fat will not be used up entirely and can be kept for another time.*

Boil potatoes in their skins. Peel and mash. Let them cool and add eggs, salt, pepper and flour. Form small croquettes, about 2 inches long. Using a small, deep saucepan, heat fat until smoking slightly. If a thermometer is used, heat to 360° F. It is important to have the fat the right temperature as in deep frying the fat must not penetrate the fried food and make it heavy and soggy. Put in not more than 2 or 3 croquettes at a time, either in or without a frying basket, and let them cook for a few minutes when they should come to the surface and have a golden colour. If no frying basket was used, take out with a perforated spoon and dry surplus fat by putting croquettes on kitchen or tissue paper. Heat the fat before you put in the next batch. Serve hot with either meat or vegetables.

Mixed vegetables (summer) *(Bukiet z jarzyn (letni)*

6 Servings

8 oz. carrots	6 eggs
1 lb. cauliflower	3 oz. butter
8 oz. peas	2 oz. dried breadcrumbs
8 oz. tomatoes	1 tablespoon chopped
8 oz. wax beans	dill or parsley
1 lb. new potatoes	salt
or potato balls	

Scrape carrots and slice thinly or if very small, leave whole. Cut off leaves of cauliflower and soak in salt water for 20 minutes. Shell peas. Dip tomatoes into boiling water and peel. Cut and remove seeds. If beans are young no stringing is necessary but if they are old string and slice. Scrape new potatoes. If old ones are used, scoop out small balls the size of a walnut.

Boil vegetables separately in as little salt water as possible. Hard-boil the eggs and shell.

This dish is very popular in Poland. Its name, a 'bouquet of vegetables', is appropriate, as the different colours of the vegetables, arranged on a large round dish or on individual plates, look like the spokes of a wheel. This is a main dish.

Fry breadcrumbs in half the butter till golden. Arrange strained hot vegetables on a large round heated dish, varying the colours as much as possible. Put the eggs in the centre. Cover the cauliflower and beans with breadcrumbs and pour melted butter over the other vegetables. Sprinkle finely chopped dill or parsley over the vegetables without crumbs.

Potato fritters *(Placki kartoflane)*

4 Servings

    1 lb. potatoes   salt
    3 oz. fat

Peel potatoes and grate on a fine grater. Put into bowl and let stand for 15 minutes. Put on a cloth and squeeze out liquid. Melt fat in frying pan and put a large spoonful of potato into hot fat, pressing it down flat. When golden on one side, turn and fry on the other. Sprinkle with salt and serve hot with vegetables or meat.

Salads dressed with cream *(Surówki zaprawiane śmietaną)*

1. 8 oz. carrots $\frac{1}{4}$ pint thin cream
    2 apples   salt
    1 tablespoon   pinch sugar
      horseradish   sprigs parsley

Scrape and grate carrots. Peel and grate apples. Peel and grate horseradish or use grated horseradish from bottle. Mix all together with cream and add seasoning to taste. Decorate with sprigs of parsley.

2. 8 oz. carrots   salt
    1 small root celeriac finely chopped parsley
    juice $\frac{1}{2}$ lemon $\frac{1}{4}$ pint soured cream

Scrape and grate carrots. Peel half the celeriac (the other half can be used for soup) and grate finely. Add all the other ingredients.

101

Sweet-sour cabbage *(Kapusta świeża na kwaśno)*

4 Servings

2 lb. cabbage	2 teaspoons salt
2 onions	½ teaspoon pepper
2 tablespoons vinegar	1 tablespoon sugar
2 tablespoons oil	1 tablespoon flour

Slice cabbage thinly. Chop onions and add all other ingredients except flour. Put just enough boiling water over it to cover, but not more. Simmer until tender (depending on the quality of the cabbage and the time of the year this can take from 30 to 45 minutes but not more). Pour off a little of the liquid and add to flour, stirring well to prevent lumps. Return to the saucepan and cook for another 10 minutes.

Variation: Chopped and fried bacon may be added.

Swedes *(Brukiew)*

6 Servings

2 large swedes	¼ pint stock or water
(about 2 lb.)	1½ teaspoons salt
1 oz. butter	2 teaspoons flour

Peel swedes and dice. Melt butter and cook swedes covered in this for 10 minutes. Add stock and salt and cook for 20 minutes. Add a little of the liquid to the flour, stir well, add and allow 5 more minutes. Serve as they are or mash.

Tomato salad *(Surówka z pomidorów)*

4–5 Servings

1 lb. tomatoes
½ teaspoon salt
1½ tablespoons vinegar

3 tablespoons oil
1 tablespoon chives

Wash tomatoes and slice thinly. Sprinkle with salt. Mix vinegar and oil and pour over tomatoes. Sprinkle with finely chopped chives.

Variations:

1. Add 1 finely chopped onion and ½ teaspoon sugar.

2. 8 oz. tomatoes
   8 oz. cucumbers
   1½ tablespoons vinegar
   3 tablespoons oil
   salt
   pepper
   2 teaspoons finely chopped dill

Wash and slice tomatoes. Peel cucumbers (ridge cucumbers are quite suitable for this salad) and slice thinly. Mix vinegar and oil, pour over tomatoes and cucumbers. Add salt and pepper and sprinkle with chopped dill.

Rainbow-coloured mashed potatoes *(Purée z kartofli w tęczowych kolorach)*

6 Servings

3 lb. potatoes	3 hard-boiled egg yolks
¼ pint milk	1 oz. butter
3 tablespoons cooked spinach	2 oz. dried breadcrumbs
	salt
1 finely grated beetroot	pepper

Peel and cook potatoes in boiling, salted water. When ready, strain and mash. Divide in 4 parts: add sieved spinach to 1 part, beetroot to the next; rub egg yolks through sieve and add to third and leave last part its natural colour but when arranged on flat dish, put breadcrumbs, fried in butter, over it. You can either arrange it on a round dish or an oblong one, in both cases alternating colours to get either 4 or 8 sections. Serve with Polish ravioli (see page 42), or another of the side dishes. It could also be served with meat.

Potatoes with sour milk *(Kartofle z kwaśnem mlekiem)*

4 Servings

1½ lb. new potatoes	2 pints sour milk
salt	(see page 215)

Scrape potatoes and put into boiling, salted water. Cook, covered, till soft. Strain and keep hot. Serve in soup plates and put icy-cold sour milk in a jug on one table so that everybody can pour it over his hot potatoes. This is a very refreshing dish on a hot summer day — it is served as a separate course, by itself.

Fried potatoes à la capucine *(Kartofle smażone po kapucyńsku)*

4 Servings

2 lb. potatoes	4 oz. dried breadcrumbs
2 egg yolks	3 oz. fat or butter
4 tablespoons milk	

Boil potatoes in their skins. Strain, peel and cut into halves or quarters, according to size. Beat egg yolks with milk in a soup plate. Dip potatoes in this and then in breadcrumbs. Fry in fat in frying pan, turning to get potatoes golden all round.

Potato salad *(Sałata z kartofli)*

4 Servings

1½ lb. potatoes, preferably kidney potatoes	salt pepper
1 large onion	chopped fresh dill
4 tablespoons oil	or parsley
2 tablespoons vinegar	

Boil potatoes in their skins. Peel while hot and slice thinly. Chop onion finely. Put potatoes and onions in a deep bowl. Mix oil and vinegar, add salt and pepper and pour it over the potatoes. Mix carefully without mashing the potatoes. Sprinkle with parsley.

Variation: Use mustard sauce (see page 120) instead of oil and vinegar. Add 2 sticks of celery, chopped up.

Baked potatoes (Kartofle wypiekane)

6 Servings

6 large potatoes
2 teaspoons caraway
seeds

1 tablespoon salt,
preferably coarse sea
salt

Scrub potatoes but do not peel. Cut in half, lengthways.
Put caraway seed on one and salt on another plate and
dip potatoes with their cut side into both. With cut side
downwards put on to a baking sheet and bake potatoes
in a hot oven (425–450° F. or Gas mark 6–7) for 45 minutes to 1 hour, depending on the size of potatoes. Serve
with sour milk or vegetables.

Corn-on-the-cob (Kukurydza)

4 Servings

corn-on-the-cob
salt

water
butter

Allow 1 corn-on-the-cob per person, if you are serving
it as hors-d'oeuvre or savoury, or 2 if you serve it as
main dish.

The only reliable test for finding out if corn is fresh
is to press your nail into a grain. If white juice seeps out,
corn is fresh. If nothing happens, it is not.

Peel outer leaves from cob and put into boiling
salted water which should cover it. Put lid on saucepan
and simmer from 15–25 minutes, according to size of
corn. Serve with butter.

Drying mushrooms *(Suszenie grzybow)*

In Poland mushrooms are very popular and replace meat on fast days. Christmas Eve supper, at which no meat is taken, always includes mushrooms as one of the dishes. Collect medium-sized field mushrooms and brush them all over with a clean, soft brush. Spread them on a sheet of paper and expose them to sunshine and draught. Turn twice every day for three days then thread on to a piece of string and hang up to dry. (A garden shed or garage is a good place for this.) When dry and hard, keep them in a paper bag.

Side dishes

The main crops raised in Poland are rye, barley, wheat, maize and various cereals unknown to most people outside Poland. They come under the general name of *Kasza* to which the specified name of the kind is added such as *kasza krakowska, kasza hreczana, kasza jaglana,* etc. They mostly belong to the millet or buckwheat families. Used instead of rice or potatoes, they add variety to meals. They are obtainable at Polish food stores and can also be used to make cheap and tasty main dishes. It is well worth while to experiment with them.

Maize meal *(Polenta)*

4 Servings

1¼ pints water   4 oz. Parmesan, grated
pinch salt   3 oz. butter
4 oz. fine polenta

Bring salted water to the boil. Stir in polenta with a wooden spoon. Simmer for 25 minutes, stirring all the time. Add cheese and butter. Serve hot with meat and vegetables or as main dish with vegetables only.

Kasza jaglana *(Kasza jaglana)*

4 Servings

10 oz. kasza jaglana	2 teaspoons salt
1¼ pints water	2 oz. butter

Wash kasza and strain. Put into boiling, salted water and simmer, covered, for 15–20 minutes, stirring frequently without squashing kasza. When water is absorbed, add butter. Put into deep fireproof dish, cover and put it into saucepan with hot water. Bring to boil and simmer for 30 minutes. Serve with sour milk, vegetables, or sauce, or top with fried onions.

Buckwheat *(Kasza hreczana)*

4 Servings

8 oz. buckwheat	1 teaspoon salt
1 pint water	1½ oz. butter

Wash buckwheat and add to boiling, salted water. Simmer for 6 minutes, stirring carefully. Strain and put into a fireproof dish and cook in a slow oven (275–300°F. or Gas mark 1–2) for 30 minutes. Each grain must be dry and separate.

Variation: Use the same quantities as above with the addition of 1 egg white. Mix washed, dry buckwheat with egg white and spread on baking sheet. Put into a moderate oven (375°F. or Gas mark 4) for 20 minutes, stirring occasionally. Add butter to boiling, salted water and put the buckwheat into this. Let it simmer for 20 minutes. The water will be absorbed and the buckwheat should be soft.

Kasza krakowska (*Kasza krakowska*)

4 Servings

8 oz. kasza krakowska	1 teaspoon salt
1 egg white	1 oz. butter
¾ pint water	

Wash kasza. Strain and add the egg white. Mix well. Spread on a baking sheet and dry in a warm oven when this has been turned off after previous use. Break up with a fork or rolling pin. If wanted, you can store the kasza until needed, as it will keep for some time.

To cook: Bring salted water to the boil, sprinkle in kasza. Simmer, covered, for 10–15 minutes. Water should be absorbed. Put saucepan with kasza into another saucepan with boiling water to make it fluffy. Allow 20–30 minutes for this. Another alternative is to remove kasza from saucepan in which it was cooked and put it in a covered, fireproof dish. Then put this in a saucepan with water and allow 30 minutes in moderate oven. Add butter and serve hot. This kasza can be used instead of rice.

Rice (*Ryż*)

4 Servings

8 oz. rice	½ teaspoon salt
2 tablespoons oil	¾ pint water
	nut butter (optional)

Wash rice under cold, running water. Heat oil and put rice in it, stirring until the rice looks transparent (2–3 minutes). Add salt and boiling water, cover and simmer until rice is cooked and every grain is separate. If you have a hot oven, you can put the rice in when it is half cooked. In this case, add a piece of butter the size of a nut. Stir only with a fork to avoid mashing the rice. It should, altogether, not take longer than 20 minutes to cook rice.

Kasza jęczmienna *(Kasza jęczmienna)*

4 Servings

    6 oz. kasza jęczmienna*   1½ teaspoon salt
    1¼ pints water   2 oz. butter

* *This kasza should be of the consistency of rice, i.e. soft and dry when cooked. It is much smaller than rice and the grains are round.*

Wash kasza, then scald. Strain and put into boiling, salted water to which butter has been added. Lower heat immediately and cover saucepan. Simmer for about 15 minutes. All the water should have been absorbed by the kasza by then. Remove from direct heat and put into a fireproof dish. Cover and put it into a saucepan of boiling water and continue to cook it like this either on the top of the stove or in the oven. It can be served after 30–40 minutes from the time it has been cooked in double saucepan. Serve either with meat or mushroom sauce or with fried onions and a salad.

Rissoles made from kasza jeczmienna *(Kotlety z kaszy jęczmiennej)*

4 Servings

    8 oz. kasza jęczmienna   2 eggs
    1½ pints water   1½ teaspoons salt
    4 oz. mushrooms   chopped parsley
    1 small onion   2 oz. dried breadcrumbs
    4 oz. fat

Wash kasza and scald. Strain and put into boiling salted water, cover and simmer for about 15 minutes. The water should have been absorbed by the kasza by that time. Stir, then spread kasza on flat dish to cool. Wash mushrooms but do not peel. Chop up. Peel and chop onion finely. Using 1 oz. fat, fry onions till golden, add mushrooms and cook for 7–10 minutes together with onions. Add eggs and all the other ingredients including onion and mushrooms to kasza and mix well. Form rissoles, dip on both sides in breadcrumbs and fry in the rest of the fat until golden both sides. Serve hot.

Note: These rissoles are served as a main dish. A salad or sauce is eaten with them.

Potato dumplings *(Kluski kartoflane)*

4 Servings

8 oz. potatoes	salt
2 eggs	2 slices bread
4 oz. flour	1 oz. butter

Boil potatoes in their skins and peel while hot. Mash very well and add eggs, flour and salt when cooled. Cut bread in small squares and fry in butter. Add to potatoes. Form small dumplings and put, singly, into boiling, salted water in a large saucepan. Cover and let it simmer for 15 minutes. Take out with colander or sieve, being careful not to squash the dumplings. Serve with meat.

Variation:

3 rashers bacon
1 onion

Chop bacon and onion and fry together. Make the dumplings slightly larger and put a spoonful of this mixture in centre.

Kasza jęczmienna with tomato purée *(Kasza jęczmienna z pomidorami)*

6 Servings

12 oz. kasza jęczmienna	1 teaspoon salt
1¾ pints water	4 tablespoons tomato
4 oz. bacon in one piece	purée

Wash kasza, scald and put into boiling water. Cut bacon into squares and slowly fry in the frying pan. Add bacon and salt to simmering kasza, stir, cover and simmer for about 15–20 minutes. When water has been absorbed by kasza, put the saucepan into another pan with boiling water and continue simmering for another 30–40 minutes or put into a fireproof dish, put this into a pan with boiling water and simmer, covered, in a oven (375°F. or Gas mark 4) for 30–40 minutes. For the last 10 minutes add tomato purée, mix well and serve the dish hot.

Onion scones *(Placki z cebuli)*

5–6 Servings

1 oz. fresh yeast	2 eggs
2 tablespoons milk or water	2 teaspoons salt
1 lb. plain flour	1 tablespoon poppyseed (optional)
10 oz. onions	½ teaspoon pepper
4 oz. butter	

Cream yeast with lukewarm milk or water (see page 146). After 15 minutes, when bubbles are beginning to form, add to sifted flour to which you have added finely chopped or grated onions, warmed butter, and the rest of the ingredients. Knead dough well. Roll out on pastry board to less than ½ inch thickness. Using a cutter, tumbler or cup, cut out rounds. Prick over with a fork and let it rise on a greased, floured baking sheet in a warm place. Bake in a moderate oven (375°F. or Gas mark 4) for 20 minutes. Serve hot with vegetables or instead of sandwiches with tea.

Sauces

A sauce should never disguise the main dish but should stress its flavour and complement it. Polish sauces are never made with gravy powder — it is unknown in Poland. The housewife uses the sediment of the roasting tin in which the meat has been cooked as the main ingredient if a meat sauce or gravy is required.

For other sauces herbs, often home-grown, are used. Dill sauce is particularly popular, made with fresh dill. Horseradish sauce, too, freshly made, or a relish made with this root, increases the appetite. It is excellent with boiled beef and many other meat dishes. The horseradish root, of which only a small quantity will be used for one meal, can be kept fresh for a few days by standing it in a little water.

White roux *(Zaprażka biała)*

   1 oz. butter $\frac{1}{4}$ pint milk or water
   1 oz. flour

Melt butter, taking care not to allow it to brown. Add flour and stir until butter is absorbed. Add cold milk or water stirring all the time. Use this as a basis for sauces or for thickening soups and vegetables.

Golden roux *(Zaprażka rumiana)*

Use the same quantities as above, but allow the flour to go a lighter or darker brown as required. If a very dark roux is needed add caramel (see below).

Caramel *(Karmel)*

Moisten 10 lumps of sugar but do not leave in water. Put into a dry saucepan and melt until they are the right colour, but do not allow to become too dark as it will taste bitter. Add a little cold water and allow to boil until the mixture is again liquid. Put into a bottle or jar and use when required.

Anchovy butter *(Masło sardelowe)*

   4 oz. butter   4 anchovies

Soak anchovies for 1 hour. Remove bones, chop finely and pass through sieve. Cream butter and add anchovies, stirring until completely blended. Freeze and cut into small squares or rounds. Serve with any kind of hot or cold meat or on sandwiches.

Anchovy sauce (uncooked) *(Sos sardelowy)*

4 anchovies
3 hard-boiled egg yolks
1 teaspoon French
   mustard
1 tablespoon olive oil

1 oz. butter
½ teaspoon castor
   sugar
juice 1 lemon
pinch pepper

Soak anchovies for 1 hour. Remove bones and chop finely. Pass through sieve together with egg yolks. Cream mustard and oil and butter. Add lemon juice with sugar and pepper. This sauce is served with fish, venison or veal.

Caper sauce *(Sos kaparowy)*

1 oz. butter
1 oz. flour
¼ pint stock or water
1 oz. capers

1 lemon
2 lumps sugar
2 egg yolks

Make a white roux (see page 114) but use water or stock instead of milk. Add capers and allow to boil for 1 or 2 minutes then add sugar, a little grated lemon rind and the lemon juice. Before serving add egg yolks beaten in a tablespoon of cold water. Allow to thicken but not to boil. This sauce is served with steamed or boiled fish, veal and poultry.

Beetroot and horseradish relish *(Ćwikła)*

6 young beetroot
3 tablespoons freshly
   grated horseradish

1 teaspoon salt
wine vinegar

Bake the beetroot until soft. Peel and slice thinly or grate. Put into a jar with alternate layers of beetroot and horseradish and sprinkle with salt. Cover with vinegar. Store the jar in a cool place and use with meat. This relish will keep for several weeks.

115

To sour beetroot *(Kwas)*

This quantity will make 4 pints

6 beetroot	1 slice rye or wholemeal
4 pints water	bread

Peel beetroot and slice finely. Put into an earthenware pot and add lukewarm water. Put the slice of bread on top. When mould appears, remove this and the bread. The juice should be soured after 4 days but can take longer in cold weather. Strain and discard the beetroot, put juice into bottles and cover with paper. Keep cool but not in refrigerator.

When *kwas* has been added to any soup it should not be allowed to boil any more, otherwise it loses flavour and colour.

Chive sauce *(Sos szczypiorkowy)*

white roux	2 egg yolks
(see page 114)	milk
salt	bunch of chives

Make a white roux. Add salt and egg yolks and stir until smooth, adding a little milk gradually. Warm through. Chop chives finely and add before serving. Use hot or cold.

Horseradish relish *(Chrzan do przechowania)*

1 large horseradish root	1½ teaspoons salt
2–3 tablespoons wine	2 teaspoons sugar
vinegar	

Peel and finely grate horseradish. Mix with the other ingredients. If wanted for storage, put in a jar and cover with greaseproof paper. Serve with meat. This relish can be used immediately or stored for a limited period of 8–10 days according to the season.

Variation: Peel and finely grate horseradish. Add 3 tablespoons of this to ¼ pint stiffly beaten thick cream.

Horseradish sauce *(Sos chrzanowy)*

6 Servings

1 horscradish root	½ teaspoon salt
1 oz. butter	1 tablespoon lemon juice
1 oz. flour	or vinegar
½ teaspoon sugar	¼ pint yoghourt

Peel horseradish and grate on a fine grater. Add to melted butter, flour, sugar and salt and stir well for a smooth white sauce. Bring to the boil and cook until it thickens. Add lemon juice or vinegar and stir well. Lastly add the yoghourt. Do not boil any more. Serve hot or cold.

Dill sauce *(Sos koperkowy)*

4 Servings

1 oz. butter	pinch salt
1 oz. flour	1 tablespoon finely
½ pint milk	chopped dill

Melt butter and stir in flour until smooth. Remove from heat and add hot but not boiling milk by the spoonful, stirring all the time. When half the milk has been used, up return to the heat, add the rest and cook for 3 minutes. Add freshly chopped dill but do not boil any more, as it would lose its colour and aroma.

117

Lemon sauce (Sos cytrynowy)

1 oz. butter	1½ lemons
1 oz. flour	parsley
½ pint stock	2 egg yolks
5 or 6 mushrooms	small pat butter

Cream butter with flour and add stock. Bring to the boil. Add mushrooms and finely grated lemon rind and simmer for 10 minutes. Add lemon juice and parsley. Cream egg yolks with the pat of butter and add to the sauce. Heat through but do not boil. This sauce is served with fish, poultry, brains or poached or hard-boiled eggs.

Mayonnaise (Majonez)

4 Servings

1 egg yolk	juice of ½ lemon
½ pint good salad oil	½ teaspoon salt

Separate the egg carefully. No white part must be attached to the yolk, as mayonnaise will not succeed otherwise. Add oil, drop by drop, beating with a wooden spoon in one direction only. When the mayonnaise begins to thicken, add lemon juice and continue to beat. Add salt and if the mayonnaise is too thick, thin it with a tablespoon of vinegar or additional lemon juice. Some people like a dash of sugar in their mayonnaise; this can be added together with the last liquid. Serve cold.

False mayonnaise (Majonez fałszywy)

1½ oz. butter	1 teaspoon French
1½ oz. flour	mustard
½ pint clear	½ teaspoon salt
stock	¼ pint oil
1 egg yolk	juice of 1 lemon

Make white sauce (see page 114) of first 3 ingredients. Let cool and add yolk, mustard and salt. Whisk with egg whisk and gradually add oil, very slowly at first, whisking it in drop by drop. Lastly add lemon juice. This is a cheap and easy sauce for salads.

Quick mayonnaise *(Sos majonezowy na prędce)*

4 Servings

1 egg, whole	$\frac{1}{2}$ teaspoon salt
3 tablespoons oil	$\frac{1}{2}$ teaspoon sugar
2 tablespoons vinegar	

Put egg, 1 tablespoon oil, 1 tablespoon vinegar, salt and sugar into a basin. Stir well with wooden spoon. Put the basin over a saucepan containing boiling water and stir or whisk until the mayonnaise thickens. Remove from the heat and gradually add 2 tablespoons oil and 1 tablespoon vinegar, stirring all the time. This mayonnaise is foolproof and cannot go wrong.

Mushroom sauce *(Sos grzybkowy)*

8 oz. mushrooms	1 tablespoon flour
1 onion	3 tablespoons milk
$1\frac{1}{2}$ oz. butter	$\frac{1}{4}$ pint soured cream
salt	or yoghourt
pinch pepper	

Wash and slice the mushrooms but do not peel. Chop the onion finely and cook in melted butter till golden. Add mushrooms, salt and pepper and cover saucepan tightly, allowing mushrooms to simmer slowly in their own juice for 15 minutes, stirring frequently. Blend flour with milk, add to mushrooms and allow to simmer for 10 minutes, adding a little more milk if necessary. Before serving add soured cream or yoghourt and heat through without allowing to boil.

Mustard sauce *(Sos musztardowy)*

¼ pint thin cream
1 oz. flour
2 egg yolks
1–2 tablespoons French
  mustard

1 teaspoon sugar
¼ teaspoon salt
pinch pepper
1 tablespoon vinegar

Put cream and flour into a small saucepan to make white sauce. Stirring all the time, let cook for 5 minutes and gradually add all the other ingredients. Serve either hot or cold.

Polish sauce *(Sos polski, szary)*

4–5 Servings

1 small onion
1½ oz. butter
1 oz. flour
½ pint fish or meat stock
2 oz. honey cake
  (optional)*

¼ pint red wine
1½ oz. sultanas
1½ oz. chopped almonds
2 teaspoons sugar
2 tablespoons water
juice of ½ lemon

* *obtainable at continental food stores*

Peel onion and chop finely. Fry lightly in butter, add flour and let it get golden coloured. Remove from heat and gradually add use fish or meat stock according to the dish with which you intend to serve the sauce. When all is absorbed return to heat and add crushed honey cake. Allow to boil until smooth. If there are lumps, pass through a sieve. Add wine, 1 teaspoon sugar, washed sultanas, and almonds. Make caramel with rest of sugar by letting it get light brown in frying pan, then adding water and allowing it to boil for 3 minutes. Lastly add lemon juice to taste. It should be sweet-sour and is eaten with fish or tongue.

Sharp sauce for cold meat *(Ostry sos do zimnego mięsa)*

4 Servings

3 hard-boiled egg yolks
1 teaspoon sugar
2 teaspoons vinegar
½ soup cube for
  consommé

¼ pint water
4 teaspoons French
  mustard
3 small pickled
  cucumbers

Pass egg yolks through sieve and cream with sugar and vinegar. Dissolve soup cube in boiling water and allow to cool. Add mustard to egg cream. Add chopped cucumbers, and gradually mix with soup. Chill and serve very cold.

Dried mushroom sauce *(Sos ze suszonych grzybów)*

4 Servings

2 oz. dried mushrooms*
¾ pint water
golden roux
  (see page 114)

salt
pepper
3 tablespoons soured
  cream or yoghourt

* *obtainable at Polish or continental shops, also at food departments of stores*

Wash mushrooms well in warm water. Soak overnight in ¾ pint water. Next day cook in same water till soft. Strain and keep liquid. Add this as well as salt and pepper to taste to golden roux and simmer for 10 minutes. Chop mushrooms finely (or cut them with kitchen scissors), add to sauce and heat through. Lastly add soured cream and heat, but do not allow to boil. This sauce can be served with boiled brisket, rissoles, potato croquettes and other dishes.

Sauce tartare *(Sos tatarski)*

mayonnaise (see page 118)
5 teaspoons French
  mustard
2 small pickled
  cucumbers

1 tablespoon capers
1 teaspoon chopped
  spring onion
1 tablespoon lemon
  juice

Chop cucumbers and capers very finely. Add these and other ingredients to small part of mayonnaise, stirring well. When mixed, gradually add the rest of the mayonnaise. Serve cold.

Sauce uncooked for venison *(Sos z dziczyzną)*

1 teaspoon made
  mustard
1 tablespoon French
  mustard
2 tablespoons rosehip
  or crab-apple jam

½ pint red wine
juice 1 lemon
2 teaspoons castor
  sugar
1 teaspoon salt

Cream mustards with jam and thin with wine and lemon juice. Add sugar and salt and mix well.

Puddings and desserts

In Poland the main meal of the day will usually end with a pudding, though this may often take the form of yeast or other pastry. Steamed puddings are also popular, and are sometimes served with raspberry juice, obtainable in bottles if not bottled at home. The various Kaszas also lend themselves for puddings and Kasza jaglana cooked in milk as well as Kasza manna (very similar to semolina) are given to babies. No recipe is given for Kasza manna, as it is used in exactly the same way as semolina in semolina pudding.

During the summer various kinds of Kisiel made of fruit juice are very much liked. This is a fruit jelly; if you use potato flour instead of cornflour or gelatine and fresh juice of the fruit in season, it makes a particularly tasty pudding.

Apple foam *(Krem z jabłek)*

4 Servings

1 lb. cooking apples
2 egg whites
3 tablespoons sugar

juice ½ lemon
3 tablespoons jam

For decorating:

6 sponge fingers

few glacé cherries

Bake apples until soft. Remove cores and sieve pulp. Whisk egg whites till very stiff, add sugar and continue whisking. Add all other ingredients including apples, and whisk for 30 minutes, or longer if possible. Put into a glass dish and decorate with halved sponge fingers and cherries.

Apple mousse *(Mus z jabłek)*

4 Servings

1 lb. apples
4 oz. icing sugar
3 egg whites
½ oz. gelatine

1 tablespoon water
juice ½ lemon
cochineal

Peel and core apples and grate. Gradually add sugar, stiffly beaten egg whites, gelatine dissolved in water (see page 11) and lemon juice. Add a drop of colouring to make the mousse pink. Allow to set. Serve very cold, decorated with sponge fingers or a little whipped cream.

Apple fritters à la polonaise (*Jabłka smażone w cieście*)

4 Servings

1 lb. cooking apples	4 oz. flour
2 eggs	1 tablespoon cornflour
1½ oz. sugar	4 oz. fat for frying
5 tablespoons milk or thin cream	icing sugar

Peel and core apples. Slice them thinly. Cream egg yolks with sugar, add milk, stiffly beaten egg whites and sieved flours. Mix very lightly. Take a slice of apple on a fork and dip in batter. Fry in a little fat on both sides till golden. Serve on a hot dish with icing sugar sieved over fritters.

Apple crumble (*Legumina z jabłek, z kruszonką*)

4 Servings

4–5 large cooking apples (about 2 lb.)	1 teaspoon powdered cinnamon
3 oz. sugar	2 tablespoons sultanas

To cover:

5 oz. flour	4 oz. brown sugar
4 oz. butter	

Peel apples and cut each into 8 pieces. Core and put into a well greased fireproof dish about 8 inches in diameter. Sprinkle sugar, cinnamon and sultanas over the apples.

Put the ingredients for covering on a pastry board and work with your fingertips to achieve the consistency of very large breadcrumbs. Sprinkle over apples and bake for 35 minutes in a moderately hot oven (400°F. or Gas mark 5). Serve hot with cream.

Apples in vanilla cream *(Nadziewane jabłka w kremie)*

4 Servings

4 or 8 cooking apples, according to size	jam
1–2 tablespoons sugar	vanilla cream
¼–½ pint water	(see below)

Peel whole apples and core, leaving bottom of apple in place to prevent jam running out. Bring water with sugar to boil in a small saucepan. Put in 1 apple at a time and simmer, turning it over after a few minutes. (Good cookers become soft very quickly but must not be allowed to get too soft.) Take out and fill hollow with jam. When all the apples are cooked and filled with jam, place them, side by side, in a deep dish. Make vanilla cream, see below. Pour cream over apples and serve very cold.

Vanilla cream *(Krem waniliowy)*

Custard powder is unknown in Poland and flavouring essences are very little used. The housewife relies on natural flavourings and the vanilla pod belongs to these. It is economical as it can be used several times and also flavours the icing sugar in which it is kept. (See vanilla pod, page 11).

¾ pint milk	3 oz. sugar
½ vanilla pod	3 yolks

Slice open vanilla pod, put it into milk, add sugar and bring to the boil. Simmer for 3 minutes. Pour a little of the milk over yolks, whisk and add to milk. Return to heat and allow the mixture to thicken without boiling, whisking or stirring all the time. Remove vanilla pod for re-use (see page 11).

126

Apple rice *(Ryż z jabłkami)*

6 Servings

12 oz. Carolina rice	5 oz. sugar
2 oz. butter	1 teaspoon cinnamon
1 pint water	1 tablespoon icing sugar
¼ pint thin cream	1 oz. butter to grease
2 lb. cooking apples	dish

Wash rice and scald. Strain, then let it dry on a clean teacloth. Melt butter and add rice, stirring with a fork until glassy. Add boiling water and simmer for 10 minutes. Test one grain if soft, otherwise allow another few minutes. Let cool. Add cream and mix. Grease fireproof dish and put in a layer of rice, then a layer of peeled, cored, thinly sliced apples. Mix sugar with cinnamon and sprinkle over apples. Repeat rice and apples and finish with rice. Dab with the rest of the butter. Bake in a moderate oven (375° F. or Gas mark 4) for 20–30 minutes. Sieve icing sugar over the dish and serve hot.

Egg noodle pudding *(Łazanki z serem)*

4–5 Servings

1 packet egg noodles	2 oz. butter
8 oz. curd cheese	2 egg yolks
2 oz. sugar	2 oz. breadcrumbs
	extra butter

Boil noodles in salted water till soft, then strain. Pass cheese through sieve. Cream sugar, butter and egg yolks and add to cheese. Grease a fireproof dish and put in layers of noodles, alternating with layers of cheese mixture. Cover with breadcrumbs and dot with a little butter. Bake in a moderate oven (357° F. or Gas mark 4) for 30 minutes. Serve with cream and sugar.

Egg noodle pudding with poppy seeds (Łazanki z makiem)

6 Servings

1 packet egg noodles $\frac{1}{4}$ pint milk
(8 oz.)   3 oz. sugar
4 oz. poppy seed

Boil noodles in salted water until soft. Strain. Bring milk to boil and cook sugar and poppy seed in it for 10 minutes. Stir this into noodles and serve hot, with extra sugar served separately.

Caramel pudding (Budyń karamelowy)

6 Servings

6 eggs $\frac{1}{4}$ vanilla pod
1 pint milk   (see page 11)
$2\frac{1}{2}$ oz. sugar   1 tablespoon rum
                      (optional)

For caramel:

5 oz. sugar

Beat eggs and add gradually all the other ingredients. Allow to stand for 30 minutes. Meanwhile make the caramel by dissolving sugar on a low heat until golden. Pour this into a ring form or pudding basin and turn it all the time to coat evenly. Fill with egg mixture and simmer in a double saucepan on a very low heat for 1 hour. Allow to cool before turning it out and serve very cold.

Hazel-nut pudding *(Budyń z orzechów)*

6 Servings

¼ pint milk	3 oz. castor sugar
1 teaspoon instant	2 oz. chocolate
coffee	3 oz. hazelnuts
3 oz. dried breadcrumbs	3 eggs

Heat milk and add coffee. Stir and soak breadcrumbs in this. Leave until all the liquid is absorbed. Add sugar, grated chocolate and roasted, ground hazelnuts. Add egg yolks and stir well. Whisk egg whites very stiUy and fold in. Steam in a greased, floured 2-pint pudding basin for 1 hour. Turn out and serve hot with cream or custard.

Honey or syrup sauce for puddings *(Sos miodowy do budyni)*

3 tablespoons water	¼ pint thin cream
4 tablespoons honey or	2 tablespoons whipped
3 tablespoons golden	thick cream
syrup	

Bring water and honey to boil and simmer for 5 minutes. Remove and stir until it thickens. Slowly add thin cream and lastly the thick cream.

Pudding of kasza jaglana

4 Servings

8 oz. kasza jaglana
(see page 108)
1¼ pints milk
1 oz. butter
4 eggs
1 oz. almonds, chopped
2 oz. sugar
2 oz. sultanas

3 tablespoons juice of
Morello cherries
1 oz. breadcrumbs
1 oz. butter to grease
dish
½ pint double cream
1 tablespoon icing sugar

Boil washed and strained kasza in milk like kasza jaglana with apples] (see below). When cooked, allow to cool. Cream egg yolks with sugar, add almonds and sultanas and add to kasza. Mix well. Fold in fruit juice and stiffly beaten egg whites. Butter and breadcrumb a deep fireproof dish and three-quarters fill with mixture. Cover well and put into a saucepan with hot water. Bring to the boil, lower heat immediately and simmer for 45 minutes. Turn out on to a hot dish and serve with whipped cream, to which sugar has been added.

Kasza jaglana with apples

4–5 Servings

12 oz. kasza jaglana
(see page 108)
1½ pints milk
1½ oz. butter
2 lb. cooking apples
5 oz. sugar

1 teaspoon cinnamon

1 oz. butter to grease
dish
1 oz. breadcrumbs

Wash kasza, strain and put into boiling milk. Cover and simmer for 15–20 minutes, stirring frequently. Peel apples and grate on coarse grater. Add sugar and cinnamon to apples. Grease fireproof dish well and sprinkle with breadcrumbs. Put in alternate layers of kasza and apples, ending with kasza. Put into a medium oven

(375° F. or Gas mark 4) and bake for 30 minutes. Serve hot with fruit juice, vanilla cream (see page 126) or thin cream.

Marrow or pumpkin pudding *(Budyń z dyni)*

6 Servings

2 lb. marrow or pumpkin	2 oz. almonds, peeled and chopped
½ teaspoon salt	4 eggs
1 pint water	3 oz. sugar
2 oz. butter	3 oz. dried breadcrumbs

Peel marrow, remove seeds, cut into squares and cook in boiling salted water. Melt the butter and fry almonds for a few minutes. Cream egg yolks with sugar, whisk egg whites until stiff and add all the ingredients to the strained and sieved marrow. Put into a greased, breadcrumbed pudding basin and cover well. (The basin should be only three-quarters full.) Steam for 1 hour. Serve hot with vanilla cream (see page 126).

Semolina cream *(Mus z manny)*

4 Servings

4 oz. semolina	pinch salt
1 pint milk	¼ pint thick cream
4 oz. sugar	angelica
	glacé cherries

Mix semolina with ½ pint milk. Bring the other ½ pint to the boil, add semolina mixture, sugar and salt and simmer on a low heat, stirring all the time, for about 7 minutes. Let it get cold. Whisk the cream until stiff and fold into the mixture. Decorate with angelica and glacé cherries.

131

Pancakes *(Naleśniki)*

4 Servings

6 oz. flour	1 egg white
pinch salt	2 egg yolks
¼ pint milk	2 tablespoons fat
¼ pint water	jam icing sugar

Sieve flour and salt into bowl. Mix milk and water in a jug. Make a hollow in the centre of the flour and drop in egg and yolks. Stir with a wooden spoon, adding liquid in small quantities until the batter is of the consistency of thick cream. Whisk with an egg whisk until bubbles appear and add the rest of the liquid, whisking it in. Set aside for at least 1 hour, preferably longer.

Melt fat in frying pan and pour it into a cup or small saucepan, keeping it warm on the stove. Leave only enough fat on the frying pan to cover it thinly. Turn the batter into a jug. Using a soup ladle (not quite full) pour the batter on to smoking hot fat in pan, removing it for this moment from the heat and quickly tilting the pan to cover it thinly and evenly. Return to heat (it should only have been away for a moment) and cook for about 1–1½ minutes. Turn over with a palette knife. Cook quickly on the other side and put it on to plate standing over boiling water on stove. Cover with a lid and continue with the next pancake. Fill each pancake with jam, sprinkle with icing sugar and serve hot. Here are three suggestions for other fillings:

Cheese filling for pancakes:

8 oz. curd cheese	grated rind of ½ lemon
2 eggs	2 tablespoons sultanas
2 tablespoons sugar	

Pass cheese through a sieve. Cream egg yolks with sugar and add to cheese. Add lemon rind. Wash the sultanas and boil them for 5 minutes in a little water. Strain, let cool and add. Whisk egg whites stiffly and fold in.

132

Hazel-nut filling for pancakes:

4 oz. hazelnuts, roast and ground
2 oz. castor sugar

juice and grated rind $\frac{1}{2}$ orange
1 tablespoon cream

Mix all ingredients.

Chocolate filling for pancakes:

4 oz. bar plain chocolate

1 oz. butter

Melt chocolate over boiling water and cream with butter.

Pancake tart *(Tort z naleśników)*

4 Servings

pancakes (see page 132)   jam

Do not roll up pancakes but put first at the bottom of a fireproof dish and spread with jam. Put the next pancake on top and, having prepared various pancake fillings in a smaller quantity (see above), put alternate layers of various fillings on top of each pancake.

Additional filling:

1 large apple
1 tablespoon icing sugar

$\frac{1}{2}$ teaspoon powdered cinnamon
few drops lemon juice
vanilla cream
(see page 126)

Peel and grate apple. Mix sugar and cinnamon and add to apple. Sprinkle with lemon juice.

When the last pancake has been put into the dish, cover with vanilla cream and put into a moderate oven (375° F. or Gas mark 4) for 20 minutes. Serve hot.

Pierogi with cherries (*Pierogi z czereśniami lub z wiśniami*)

4 Servings

    pierogi dough (see page 42)

For filling:

    1 lb. cherries, sweet or   2 oz. sugar if Morello
    Morello   cherries are used

For topping:

    2 oz. butter   2 oz. dried breadcrumbs
    sugar to serve with pierogi.

Wash and stalk cherries but leave stones. On each piece of dough put 2–3 cherries and with Morella cherries add a little sugar. Cook like Lithuanian ravioli (see page 81). Melt butter and fry breadcrumbs till golden. Pour over pierogi and serve sugar separately.

Variation: Do not use breadcrumbs as topping, only butter, and serve soured cream in a sauceboat to pour over individual helpings.

Lazy pierogi (*Leniwe pierogi*)

6 Servings

    2 boiled potatoes (8 oz.)   1 egg white
    1 lb. curd cheese   2 egg yolks
    2 oz. butter   6 oz. flour

To serve:

    2 oz. melted butter   sugar

Boil potatoes in their skins. Strain, peel and pass through sieve while still hot. Let cool and add to curd cheese. Cream butter and the egg yolks and add to mixture. Add flour and stiffly beaten white and make dough. Form a roll about 1 inch in diameter and cut into small pieces, about 1 inch long. Put carefully into boiling salted water in a large saucepan and simmer for 10 minutes uncovered. Take out one by one with a straining spoon and put on a hot plate or dish. Serve hot melted butter and sugar separately.

Sago pudding *(Budyń z kaszy)*

6 Servings

2 pints milk
pinch salt
1 oz. butter
3 tablespoons sago

2 eggs
4 oz. sugar
lemon or orange peel

Bring milk, salt and butter to the boil. Pour about 1 pint boiling water over sago and strain. Add sago to milk and simmer for 10 minutes. Stir egg yolks with sugar till foamy. Whisk egg whites stiffly and add them as well as finely grated peel to yolks. Fold into sago mixture when cooled. Put into a large fireproof dish and bake in a moderate oven (375° F. or Gas mark 4) for 20 to 25 minutes. Serve hot.

Tapioca can be used instead of sago.

Christmas Eve compote of fruit *(Kompot z owoców mieszanych)*

8 Servings

1 lb. prunes
1 lb. dried apricots
8 oz. figs
8 oz. seedless raisins

peel of 1 orange or lemon
4 oz. sugar
1 pint water
3 tablespoons rum

Wash fruit and soak overnight. Make syrup with sugar and water and simmer for 10 minutes uncovered. Add finely grated peel. Add fruit and water in which it has been soaked. The fruit should be covered. Simmer till soft (about 15 minutes). When cool add rum.

135

Chocolate mousse *(Budyń czekoladowy)*

4 Servings

1 egg
7 oz. sugar
4 tablespoons cocoa
¼ pint single cream

½ oz. gelatine
2 tablespoons water
¼ pint thick cream

Beat egg, sugar, cocoa and single cream on top of a double saucepan until it thickens. Remove from heat and add gelatine dissolved in water (see page 11). Put back over heat and whisk until gelatine is well blended. Fold in stiffly beaten cream and pour mixture into a mould rinsed in cold water. Keep in a cold place for 3 hours before turning out.

Coffee cream *(Krem kawowy)*

4 Servings

2 egg whites
4 egg yolks
¼ pint strong black coffee
¼ pint thin cream

1 tablespoon cornflour
1 tablespoon rum (optional)
4 oz. hazel nuts
thick cream (optional)

Whisk eggs, coffee and cream, into which you have stirred the cornflour, over a low heat until the mixture thickens. Roast hazel nuts in the oven until the skin starts cracking and the nuts begin to colour (about 15 minutes). Chop nuts and add them and rum to cream. Serve in small glasses. If wanted, put a teaspoon of whisked, double cream on top of each glass.

Cranberry jelly *(Kisiel z żurawin)*

4 Servings

8 oz. cranberries	½ stick cinnamon
1½ pint water	1 tablespoon cornflour
12 oz. sugar	1 tablespoon cold water
2 cloves	

Put cranberries into boiling water and simmer for 30 minutes or until soft. Pass through a sieve together with water. Add sugar and spices and bring again to boil. Simmer for 10 minutes. Cream cornflour with cold water and gradually add some of the hot liquid. Return all to a saucepan and simmer for 3 minutes. Put into a mould rinsed with cold water. Turn out when set. Serve with cream.

Lemon mousse *(Krem cytrynowy)*

4 Servings

2 eggs	½ oz. gelatine
6 oz. sugar	2 tablespoons water
juice and rind ½ lemon	¼ pint thick cream

Beat egg yolks and sugar until foamy. Add lemon juice and finely grated rind. Put gelatine into water and dissolve over gentle heat, stirring constantly but not allowing to boil. Add to egg mixture and whisk all together. Whisk egg whites and, separately, whisk cream. Fold both into mixture gently, keeping a little of the cream for decorating. Put mixture into a mould rinsed in cold water. Keep in a cold place for 3 hours before turning out. Decorate with cream.

Orange salad *(Kompot z pomarańcz)*

6 Servings

6 oranges	4 oz. sugar
3 apples	$\frac{1}{4}$ pint water
1 tablespoon lemon juice	

Pour boiling water over the oranges and discard water. Peel the oranges and slice very thinly. Remove all pips. Peel apples, slice also very thinly and remove the core. Let them stand with lemon juice for a few minutes. Arrange orange and apple slices alternately in serving dish. Bring sugar in water to the boil and simmer for 10 minutes. Let cool and pour over fruit. If wanted, a tablespoon of brandy or kirsch can be added.

Orange cream *(Krem pomarańczowy)*

4 Servings

2 eggs	2 tablespoons lemon juice
$3\frac{1}{2}$ oz. sugar	
grated orange peel*	$1\frac{1}{2}$ leaves gelatine
6 tablespoons orange juice	1 tablespoon water
	$\frac{1}{4}$ pint thick cream

To decorate:

$\frac{1}{8}$ pint double cream

* *only the yellow part of the peel must be grated as otherwise it is bitter*

Whisk egg yolks with sugar and peel until foamy. Strain juices and add. Dissolve gelatine in water (see page 11) and add, stirring until cold but still runny. Whisk egg whites and cream and fold into mixture. Put into a glass bowl and let it stand in a cold place. Decorate with whipped cream.

Redcurrant jelly *(Kisiel)*

4 Servings

   1 lb. redcurrants   6 oz. sugar
   1 pint water   1 oz. cornflour

Wash and stalk redcurrants and bring to boil in water. Simmer covered for 10 minutes and strain. Take off a little of the liquid, and cool. Add sugar to the rest and bring to the boil. Cream cornflour with cooled juice and add to boiling liquid. Reduce heat and while stirring all the time let simmer for 2 or 3 minutes. When cold, serve with cream.

Stewed pears *(Kompot z gruszek)*

4 Servings

   2 lb. pears   1 pint water
   4 oz. sugar   2 tablespoons lemon juice

Peel pears and either halve or leave whole, according to size. Bring sugar and water to the boil and simmer for 10 minutes. Add pears, cover and simmer until soft. Remove from heat and add lemon juice. Serve cold.

Variation: Add ½ stick of cinnamon to water at the beginning of boiling. Remove this at the end and omit lemon juice.

Pears in caramel *(Gruszki w karamelu)*

6 Servings

6 large pears	1 pint water
6 oz. sugar	¼ pint thick cream

Peel pears but do not discard peel. Remove stalks and halve pears, removing core. Dissolve sugar on its own on very low heat until it is golden. Meanwhile cook washed peel in water for 10 minutes, then remove peel and discard, keeping the liquid. Add this water to caramel and cook pears in it till soft. Put pears into dish and measure liquid. Use ½ pint of this and cover pears with it.

Variation: Use canned pears instead and mix caramel with the juice instead of using water.

Pears Hélène *(Gruszki w sosie czekoladowym)*

4 Servings

1 large can pears (2 lb.)

For covering:

juice from can	2 eggs
4 oz. plain chocolate	2 oz. sugar
1 tablespoon cornflour	

Strain pears and arrange in serving dish. Heat ½ pint pear juice and melt chocolate in it. Mix cornflour with 2 tablespoons pear juice, add to chocolate mixture and let simmer for 5 minutes. Beat eggs in a bowl. Gradually add chocolate mixture to them and return to saucepan. Add sugar and bring to the boil. Remove from heat. Allow chocolate sauce to cool and pour over pears.

Bombes

A bombe is one of the most delicious and rich sweets. The name comes from the shape of the mould and it is essential that the right mould is used to get proper results. It is also important to use the right size of mould, as it should be filled up to the top.

To make bombes

When making a bombe you will need enough ice to surround and cover the mould put into a bucket. The ice must be chopped finely and about 8 oz – 1 lb. rock salt should be mixed with the ice to prevent it from melting. A coarsely woven cloth, wrung out with cold water, covering the top of the bucket, will also help to keep the ice hard. Naturally the bucket must be kept in a cold place.

When filling the mould with the mixture, cover the top with a round of greaseproof paper. Put the lid on the bombe and seal edges so that no drop of salt water can seep in. To do this, either cover the edge of the lid, where it meets the tin, with a thick layer of fat or with flour paste, sealing it hermetically. Then bury the mould in the bucket, surrounded and covered with ice. Allow 4–5 hours for freezing; now the most dangerous moment has come, when many a delicious bombe is spoiled, the turning out. Remove the mould from bucket and rinse well with cold water on the outside. Remove fat or dough from the edges carefully, wash your hands, as salt water might cling to them, and dry the mould outside. Dip the rounded end of the mould into warm (not hot) water, take out and remove lid. With a long-bladed or palette knife go around the edges of the bombe to loosen it. Put a flat glass dish on top of the mould, after having removed the paper covering the bombe, turn it upside down, and the bombe will slide on to the dish. Instead of dipping the mould, a cloth, wrung out with hot water, can be wrapped round it for a moment before turning out the bombe.

Royal bombe (Bomba królewska)

12 Servings

8 egg yolks	1 pint thick cream
12 oz. sugar	4 oz. chocolate drops
inside of ½ vanilla pod	8 oz. candied fruit
(see page 11)	

Whisk egg yolks, 4 oz. sugar and vanilla until light-coloured and thick. Whisk the cream until stiff and whisk in rest of sugar. Add egg mixture to cream by the spoonful, whisking all the time, until all is blended. Keep some chocolate drops for decoration and fold the rest into the cream. Chop candied fruit and add, also keeping some for decoration. Rinse the bombe mould with cold water, fill and continue as described on page 141. When turned out, decorate with chocolate drops and fruit.

Caramel bombe (Bomba karamelowa)

6 Servings

7 oz. lump sugar	4 egg yolks
½ pint milk	¾ pint thick cream
4 oz. castor sugar	

Melt sugar on a slow heat until light golden, add milk and simmer until sugar is completely melted. Whisk

142

the castor sugar with egg yolks until light-coloured and foamy, then gradually add the cooled caramel mixture.

Whisk cream stiffly and slowly add the other mixture to the cream, whisking all the time. Rinse the bombe mould with cold water and fill. Continue as described on page 141.

Chocolate bombe *(Bomba czekoladowa)*

6 Servings

$\frac{1}{4}$ pint thin cream	4 oz. sugar
6 oz. chocolate,	4 egg yolks
preferably bitter	$\frac{1}{2}$ pint thick cream

Put cream, melted chocolate, sugar and egg yolks into a double saucepan and whisk until the mixture begins to thicken. Whisk cream stiffly, fold into cooled chocolate mixture and fill the bombe mould, previously rinsed with cold water, with one mixture. Continue as described on page 141.

Coffee cream bombe *(Bomba kawowa)*

12 Servings

4 tablespoons instant	5 egg yolks
coffee	5 oz. sugar
$\frac{1}{2}$ pint boiling water	1 pint thick cream

Make strong coffee with boiling water. Let it cool. Whisk egg yolks and sugar in a double saucepan and gradually add coffee; whisk until mixture begins to thicken. Let it cool. Whisk cream stiffly and carefully fold into coffee cream.

Rinse the bombe mould with cold water and fill. Continue as described on page 141.

Peach bombe *(Bomba z brzoskwin)*

6 Servings

    1 lb. peaches   5 oz. sugar
    juice 1 lemon   ¾ pint thick cream

Rub the peaches, uncooked, through a sieve. Add lemon juice. Cream with sugar. Whisk cream stiffly and gradually fold in the peach mixture, whisking all the time. Rinse the bombe mould with cold water and fill. Continue as described on page 141.

Pineapple bombe *(Bomba ananasowa)*

12 Servings

    1 large can pineapple   5 oz. sugar
        pieces   juice 1 lemon
    7 egg yolks   1 pint thick cream

Strain pineapple. In a double saucepan whisk ½ pint pineapple juice, egg yolks, sugar and lemon juice until the mixture begins to thicken. Whisk cream stiffly. Add to cooled pineapple mixture. Add drained pineapple, folding it in carefully. Rinse the bombe mould with cold water, fill with mixture and continue as described on page 141.

Yeast cookery

Yeast is an important item in Polish cooking. Baking powder, self-raising flour or baking soda are hardly used at all. Yeast dishes, both as sweets and savouries, are very popular and the variety of recipes covers a wide range — from breads and everyday foods to rich pastries.

Bread, to the Pole, means more than any other food. He has often had to go without it through wars and famine, and 'give us each day our daily bread' has never become an empty phrase with him. Bread, as a symbol, is served together with salt on a platter to a newcomer in a community. It is never wasted or thrown away and to see bread in dustbins will always hurt a Pole. If there are any left-overs, they are used in various dishes such as dump-lings etc. or for thickening sauces, or, last but not least, for breadcrumbs. For these the bread is dried in the oven and ground or crushed; if kept in a jar or paper bag the crumbs will keep for a long time.

In the country, bread is mostly baked at home. Rye bread, often soured, is very tasty. Dry yeast can be used instead of fresh yeast and its only disadvantage is that it takes longer to rise.

How to use yeast

1. Yeast is a raising agent and therefore self-raising flour, soda or baking powder must not be used.
2. Fats and liquids should be lukewarm.
3. Liquids can be either milk, water or sour milk.
4. Dried yeast needs more time to rise than fresh yeast, both during the proving and when mixed with the other ingredients.
5. Always start with the proving: crumble yeast into a bowl, add a little liquid and about 1 tablespoon flour. A teaspoon of sugar will hasten the rising. The consistency should be that of a thick batter. Let it stand in a warm place for 15–30 minutes. It should rise and make bubbles.
6. Yeast pastry can be made in two ways: either by beating with a wooden spoon until the dough is smooth and glossy and no longer sticks to spoon, or by kneading with the hands.
7. The dough must be allowed to rest covered with a porous cloth. This must be done in a warm place for 30 minutes to 1 hour, or in a cold place overnight. For a warm place use the airing cupboard,

146

a plate rack above the kitchen stove, a shelf above a radiator or a bowl with warm water. Temperature should be warm, *not* hot.

8. If the dough is filled or has a topping, it must be allowed to rise twice: once before adding the filling or topping and once with it.
9. Avoid draught both during beating and rising and when cooling after baking.
10. Yeast pastry is baked in a hot oven. The oven door must not be banged when you shut it.

Savoury pierogi *(Pierogi z bekonem)*

13 oz. flour
1 oz. yeast
¼ pint milk
1 egg yolk

4 oz. melted fat
½ teaspoon salt
milk to brush pastry

For filling:

6 oz. bacon
2 small onions

1 hard-boiled egg

Cream yeast with 1 tablespoon flour and lukewarm milk. Let stand in a warm place for 15 minutes. Mix the egg yolk with other ingredients, add yeast mixture and work the dough with your hands till smooth. Cover with a teacloth and let stand in a warm place for 1 hour. Roll out and cut in rounds with a tumbler to ¼ inch thickness. Meanwhile chop up onion and bacon, fry together, cool, add chopped egg and put a teaspoonful on each round. Fold over and press the ends together. Cut out once more to have a clean edge. Let rise for 40 minutes, brush with milk and bake in a hot oven (425–450°F. or Gas mark 6–7) for 15–20 minutes. Serve hot.

Rich yeast pastry *(Ciasto pól-francuskie)*

This pastry is similar to Danish pastry and is used both for sweets and savouries. Like puff pastry, it consists of two doughs.

For main dough:

1 oz. yeast	1 egg
8 oz. flour	¼ teaspoon salt
1 tablespoon sugar	
5 tablespoons lukewarm milk	

For second dough:

4 oz. butter or margarine	2 oz. flour

Cream yeast with 1 tablespoon flour and 1 teaspoon sugar. Put in a warm place for 15 minutes. Put the other ingredients into a bowl and when yeast mixture has risen add to bowl and beat with a wooden spoon, then work through with your hands until the dough is ready for rolling out on a pastry board.

Make the second dough by cutting fat into flour, then quickly form it into an oblong block with your hands. Roll out the first dough to ½-inch thickness, put the second dough in the centre and fold both ends of the first dough over it. From now on the pastry is treated as a single dough. Roll out into a straight strip, fold this in three and let it rest for 30 minutes in a cold place. Repeat rolling and folding three times (these are called 'turns'). After the last turn cover with a damp cloth and let it stand for several hours, preferably until the next day. If kept for this length of time give it one more turn.

Pierogi with cabbage in yeast pastry *(Pierogi ruskie ze słodką kapustą)*

6 Servings

For yeast pastry:

1 oz. yeast	2 egg yolks
¼ pint milk	¼ teaspoon salt
½ teaspoon sugar	1 oz. butter for
1 lb. flour	brushing

For filling:

1 lb. white cabbage	1 oz. butter
1 teaspoon salt	1 onion
½ teaspoon sugar	2 oz. mushrooms
¼ teaspoon pepper	1 hard-boiled egg

Cream yeast with 2 tablespoons lukewarm milk, sugar and 1 tablespoon flour. Let it stand in warm place for 15 minutes. Add to the other ingredients and beat with a wooden spoon. When the dough is smooth, cover with a teacloth and put in a warm place for rising. When double in bulk (after about 40 minutes to 1 hour) put on pastry board. Take off a piece, roll it with your hand into the shape of a sausage and cut off pieces the size of plums. Press these flat with your hand (the pieces should be round or square) and put a dessertspoon of filling in centre of each. Fold over and press edges together firmly. Brush tops with melted butter. Grease baking sheets and bake pierogi in a moderate oven (375° F. or Gas mark 4) for 30–35 minutes.

Filling: Cut cabbage into several pieces and cook in boiling water for 5 minutes. Strain and squeeze out in a teacloth to remove as much moisture as possible. Chop finely and add salt, sugar and pepper. Melt butter and fry finely chopped onion for 5 minutes. Add cabbage, cover saucepan and simmer for 15–20 minutes. Wash mushrooms and chop. Add to cabbage together with chopped egg.

Rich yeast pastry with cabbage *(Kulebiak)*

6 Servings

1 oz. yeast
1 lb. flour
1 teaspoon sugar
1 teaspoon salt

2 eggs
¼ pint milk
4 oz. butter

For filling:

1 lb. white cabbage
2 onions, chopped
3 oz. butter
4 oz. mushrooms
2 hard-boiled eggs

1½ teaspoons salt
½ teaspoon pepper
6 oz. cooked rice
1 egg for brushing
pastry

Cream yeast with 1 tablespoon flour and the sugar. Put in a warm place for 15 minutes. Put the rest of the flour into a bowl and add salt, eggs and lukewarm milk. Work the dough with your hands. When it does not stick any more cover with a teacloth and put it in a warm place to rise. When risen (after about 40 minutes) put it on pastry board and roll out into a square. Put butter in one piece in centre, fold over dough as for French pastry, roll out to double its size and fold over from both sides. Put in a cold place for 20 minutes. Roll out again and fold over as before. Repeat this rolling out and putting the dough in a cold place three times.

Meanwhile prepare filling: Pour boiling water over cabbage leaves and strain. Fry onions in butter, add chopped-up cabbage and cook slowly for 20 minutes. Add sliced mushrooms and allow another few minutes of cooking. Add sliced eggs and seasoning and stir all together. (An alternative is to keep the sliced eggs separately and put them in as a layer between the rice and cabbage.)

Now roll out pastry about ¼ inch thick to form a rectangle. Put a layer of rice over the pastry, then a layer of cabbage. Roll up like a Swiss roll. Beat egg with fork and brush over top of roll. Put in a greased, floured roasting tin and bake in a moderate oven (350–375° F. or Gas mark 3–4) for 30–40 minutes. Serve hot as a main dish.

Potato fritters with yeast *(Placki kartoflane na drożdżach)*

6 Servings

4 oz. flour	3 oz. sugar
2 lb. potatoes	2 eggs
½ pint milk	1 oz. butter
½ oz. yeast	4–5 oz. fat for frying

Sieve flour into a deep bowl. Peel potatoes and grate on a fine grater. Squeeze out through a teacloth. Heat milk to boiling point. Put aside 2 tablespoons of milk and allow to cool. Pour the rest of the milk, boiling hot, over the potatoes. Dissolve yeast in lukewarm milk and add 1 teaspoon sugar. Add the rest of the sugar to the potatoes together with egg yolks and butter. Whisk whites till stiff and add them to potatoes. Heat fat in frying pan and put dessertspoons of mixture into fat. Fry until golden. Turn once and keep hot. Serve with fruit juice such as raspberry juice (obtainable at many grocers) or with stewed fruit.

Sandwich cake *(Tort słony jako przystawka)*

10–12 Servings

1 oz. yeast
¼ pint milk
12 oz. flour
1 egg white

2 egg yolks
1 oz. butter
1 teaspoon salt

For filling:

8 oz. butter
1 can sardines
6 oz. ham
3 hard-boiled eggs

4 tablespoons cooked
  spinach
4 oz. grated cheese

For covering:

2 oz. smoked salmon
4 radishes
4 oz. thick cream

1 tablespoon grated
  horseradish

Cream yeast in 2 tablespoons lukewarm milk with 1 tablespoon flour. Allow to stand for 15 minutes. Mix all the other ingredients in a bowl, add yeast mixture and the rest of milk and beat for 10 minutes. Cover with a teacloth and let rise in a warm place until double in bulk. Grease and flour a 10-inch cake tin. Put dough into it, flatten it and cover. Let rise again. When double in bulk bake in hot oven (425°F. or Gas mark 6) for 40 minutes. Let cool. Do not cut until the next day as otherwise it will crumble.

Cut through three times so that you have four layers of cake. Cream butter until very foamy and divide into four parts.

1. Mash sardines with fork and add to one part of butter. Spread on a layer of cake.
2. Chop ham and mix with second part of butter, or spread layer with butter and put sliced ham over it. Add 1 sliced hard-boiled egg.
3. Add creamed spinach to third part of butter and

spread this on the next layer. Sprinkle with half the grated cheese. Cover with last layer.
4. Spread with butter, creamed with cheese.

Decorate as follows:

Cut salmon in strips and roll up to form roses. Put radishes in iced water after having cut through the skin. They should look like flowers. Whip cream stiffly, chop eggs and add them and horseradish to cream. Using forcing bag with pipe with a large star-shaped opening, force cream around edge of cake and make decoration in centre. The whole effect should be that of a sweet cake so that the surprise of eating a savoury cake is greater. Cut like any other cake, so slices show the different coloured fillings.

Apple dumplings *(Jabłka w cieśie)*

rich yeast pastry (see page 150)

For filling:

2 small apples per person   sultanas (a few for each
½ pint water   apple)
                        1 tablespoon sugar

icing sugar

Make yeast pastry and cut into squares, large enough to cover a whole apple.

Peel and core apples. Simmer in water with sugar in a very small saucepan and turn once. (The best way is to cook them singly, as they are soft very quickly.) Remove from water, let dry and fill the hollow with sultanas. Put an apple on each square, fold over the corners to meet in the centre and press together. Bake in a hot oven (425° F. or Gas mark 6) for 25–30 minutes. Sieve icing sugar over the dumplings before serving.

Rum baba *(Babka z rumem)*

1 oz. yeast	3 oz. butter
4 oz. sugar	lemon rind
3 tablespoons milk	4 eggs
8 oz. flour	

butter and breadcrumbs for ring mould

For covering:

4 oz. sugar	1 tablespoon lemon juice
2 tablespoons apricot jam	2 tablespoons rum or 1 teaspoon essence of rum
4 tablespoons water	

Cream yeast with sugar and add lukewarm milk. Stir until smooth and let it stand in a warm place for 15 minutes. Put flour into a basin, add melted butter, finely grated lemon rind and egg yolks. If unsalted butter or margarine is used, add a pinch of salt, but with salted butter this is not necessary. Beat well, then add yeast mixture and beaten egg whites. Continue beating until the dough is very light. Cover, put in a warm place and let stand for 1 hour. Beat it down, cover and let it rest again for 1 hour. Grease and breadcrumb a ring mould, put in dough and allow to rest for 30 minutes. Bake in a moderate oven (375° F. or Gas mark 4) for 35 minutes. Test with a wooden skewer. If it comes out clean, take baba out. Make covering by putting sugar, jam and water into a small saucepan and letting it simmer for 10 minutes. Add the other ingredients but do not allow to boil any more. Turn baba out and either pour the covering over top and sides or put it into a ring mould; return the baba to this and let it soak it in. Serve with whipped cream.

Yeast pancakes *(Bliny)*

4 Servings

4 oz. flour	½ pint milk
½ oz. yeast	½ teaspoon salt
1 teaspoon sugar	fat for frying
1 egg	

Cream 1 tablespoon 'flour with yeast and sugar and let stand for 15 minutes. Meanwhile mix the other ingredients, whisking well. When the yeast mixture has risen, add to the other ingredients and stir. It should have the consistency of pancake batter. Let it stand again in a warm place to rise (about 30–40 minutes). Heat the fat in a frying pan (preferably an iron one) until smoking hot and pour in a little batter, very thinly. Fry quickly on both sides and keep hot on a plate over boiling water. When all the batter has been used up, fill and serve. Bliny can be served as a savoury or dessert. As a savoury, you can fill them with anchovy butter (see page 114), caviar or any other savoury filling. Sprinkle hard-boiled chopped egg over the bliny.

As a sweet fill them with jam or sprinkle lemon juice over each and serve with sugar and soured cream.

Yeast buns with vanilla cream *(Buchciki z kremem waniliowym)*

These buns are eaten as a sweet. They should be freshly baked and the vanilla cream ought to be hot.

12 oz. flour	3 oz. butter
1 oz. fresh yeast	2 egg yolks
¼ pint milk	lemon or orange peel
3 oz. sugar	

For vanilla cream:

1 pint milk	½ tablespoon cornflour
3 tablespoons icing sugar	2 yolks
1 packet Vanillin or	
½ vanilla pod	

Put flour on pastry board. Cream yeast in a small basin with 2 tablespoons of the lukewarm milk and 1 teaspoon sugar. Melt butter and add two-thirds of this to flour, as well as the rest of the sugar, egg yolks and finely grated peel. Slowly add the rest of the milk, working the dough with your hands. After 10 to 15 minutes add the yeast mixture, which should have risen by then. Knead the dough until it leaves your hands. Cover with a teacloth and let it rise for 30 minutes in a warm place. Grease a 9-inch cake or baking tin. Put a little flour on the board to dust your hands with. Now pull off a small piece of dough, the size of a damson, put into cake tin and brush over the sides with the rest of the melted butter. Pull off the next bit of dough and put close to the first piece. Butter again. Continue like this until all the dough is used up and the tin full. If any space is left free in centre, put in greaseproof paper to fill it, crumpling it up. By having no space to rise sideways, the buns rise in height. The buttering at the sides is necessary to enable you afterwards to break each bun off separately. Cover the tin with a teacloth and allow to rise in a warm place until the buns are about double their size. Put into a hot oven (425–450°F. or Gas mark

6–7) and bake for 30 minutes. *Meanwhile make vanilla cream.*

Take a little of the milk and cream cornflour and yolks with it. Bring milk and sugar to boil, pour a little over egg mixture and stir well, then return this to milk and simmer for 3 minutes. Add Vanillin during this time. If a vanilla pod is used instead, see page 11. Serve hot cream with buns.

Nut roll *(Strucla drożdżowa z masą orzechową)*

9 oz. flour   ½ oz. fresh yeast
4 oz. butter   2 tablespoons milk
3 oz. sugar
icing sugar

For filling:

7 oz. sugar   ½ oz. butter
¼ pint water
14 oz. walnuts or
    hazelnuts

Put flour, butter and sugar on pastry board and make pastry. Dissolve yeast in lukewarm milk, let rise for 10 minutes and, using your hands, work it into the pastry. Leave it on pastry board for 1 hour, covered with a cloth. *To make filling:* bring sugar and water to the boil and simmer on a very low heat for 8–10 minutes. Grind nuts finely (preferably twice) and add to syrup. Remove from heat and add butter. Let cool.

Roll out pastry to less than ½-inch thickness. Put filling all over it, only leaving ends on all four sides uncovered. Roll up like Swiss roll. Brush over with milk or egg yolk (optional) and let it rest, covered, on a greased and floured baking sheet or roasting tin for 1 hour, or less if it has risen well. Bake in a hot oven (425–450° F. or Gas mark 6–7) for 10 minutes, then reduce heat and bake for 20 minutes. Let cool, sprinkle with icing sugar.

Doughnuts *(Pączki)*

3 oz. butter	¼ pint milk
2 oz. sugar	12 oz. flour
4 egg yolks	1 teaspoon rum (optional)
1 oz. fresh yeast	pinch salt
icing sugar	

For filling:

apricot jam

For frying:

8 oz. whipped-up cooking fat	8 oz. lard

Cream butter, sugar and egg yolks. Cream yeast with half of the flour and milk and put into a warm place for 15 minutes. Add to creamed mixture and gradually stir in the rest of the flour, salt and rum. Beat the dough with wooden spoon until it leaves the spoon clean. Put into a warm place covered with a napkin or teacloth for 15 minutes. Sprinkle flour on pastry board and roll out dough to the thickness of your little finger. Cut out rounds with a pastry cutter 2½ inches in diameter. Put a teaspoon of jam on one round, cover with another and press down with your fingertips so that the jam will not run out when baking. Now cut out once more, using a cutter 2 inches in diameter. Cover the baking sheet with a floured teacloth and put the doughnuts, their tops at the bottom, on to this. Cover with another cloth and put in a warm place to rise. When they are almost double their size, heat the fat in a small, deep saucepan. The right temperature of fat can be recognised when the handle of a wooden spoon, dipped first into cold water and then into fat, makes this boil around the handle. Fry doughnuts one by one and with the top of the doughnut downwards. Cover for a moment and when golden turn over and fry the other side uncovered.

Put straight away on kitchen or tissue paper to absorb surplus fat. Sieve icing sugar over doughnuts. They are at their best when eaten fresh.

False doughnuts *(Racuszki)*

8 oz. flour	$\frac{1}{4}$ pint milk
1 oz. yeast	$1\frac{1}{2}$ oz. fat
2 oz. sugar	2 eggs
icing sugar	

For frying:

4 oz. fat

Sieve flour. Cream yeast with 1 teaspoon sugar and half the milk. Let rise in a warm place for 15 minutes. Melt fat. Cream eggs with rest of sugar and add to all the other ingredients. Beat with wooden spoon until the dough shows bubbles. The dough should be the thickness of whipped cream. Cover with a teacloth and put in a warm place to rise. When double the size after about 40 minutes, put a spoonful of fat on the frying pan and heat. When smoking, put a tablespoon of dough on to the fat, reduce heat and fry until golden. Turn over and repeat. Put on kitchen or tissue paper to absorb surplus of fat. When all the dough is used up, serve warm with icing sugar sprinkled over pastry and with honey, fruit juice or jam.

Scalded yeast rolls *(Strucle parzone)*

½ pint milk	2 oz. sugar
1¼ oz. flour	finely grated lemon peel
1 oz. fresh yeast	pinch salt
3 oz. butter	egg or milk for
3 eggs	brushing

For filling:

6 oz. poppyseed*	2 oz. sultanas
2 oz. butter	1 egg
3 oz. sugar	

* obtainable at continental food shops

Heat ¼ pint milk to boiling point and pour over 4 oz. of flour, stirring well to avoid lumps. Let cool. Warm the rest of milk till lukewarm and cream yeast with 2 tablespoons of this. Let rise in a warm place for 15 minutes when it should show bubbles. Cream butter, eggs and sugar, lemon peel and salt. Add scalded flour, yeast mixture, rest of milk and flour and work the dough with your hands until it feels spongy and stops sticking to hands. Halve, roll out on a floured board to o-inch thickness, fill, roll up like a Swiss roll and let it rise in a warm place. Brush with beaten egg or milk and bake in a very moderate oven (300–350° F. or Gas mark 2–3) for 35 to 40 minutes. Take out and let cool before serving.

Filling:

Melt butter and cook all ingredients except egg in it. Allow to get cold and add egg.

Variations:

Curd cheese filling

1 lb. curd cheese	finely grated orange
3 oz. sugar	peel
2 oz. sultanas or raisins	2 eggs

Cream cheese, sugar and egg yolks. Add sultanas and peel and stiffly beaten egg whites.

Nut filling

4 oz. ground nuts or	3 oz. sugar
almonds	1 teaspoon cinnamon
2 oz. breadcrumbs	2 oz. butter

Mix all the dry ingredients. Melt butter and add, stirring well.

Plum slices *(Placek ze śliwkami)*

1 lb. flour	1½ oz. butter
½ pint milk	2 egg yolks
1 oz. yeast	1 egg
1½ oz. sugar	¼ teaspoon salt

For topping:

2 lb. plums	1 teaspoon cinnamon
2 tablespoons icing sugar	

Put half the flour into a bowl. Bring half the milk to the boil and pour over flour, stirring well to avoid lumps. Cream yeast with 1 tablespoon lukewarm milk, 1 table-spoon flour and 1 teaspoon sugar. Allow to rise for 15–20 minutes. Warm the rest of the milk with butter and add this, the rest of the flour and the sugar, yolks and egg to the flour mixture in the bowl. Beat and add salt and yeast mixture. Beat until smooth and shiny. Put in a warm place, covered with a teacloth, to rise for 40 minutes. *Prepare the topping as follows:* Wash and stalk plums. Cut open but do not divide in half. Remove stones and cut at both ends as shown in diagram. (see page 161).

Put dough into a 15 × 12-inch baking tin. Cover dough completely with plums, open side upwards. Cover with cloth and let rise once more for 1 hour. Mix sugar with cinnamon and sieve over plums. Bake in a hot oven (425–450° F. or Gas mark 6–7) for 20–25 minutes. Cut in slices.

Yeast coffee cake *(Babka drożdżowa)**

5 oz. butter	½ oz. fresh yeast
3 oz. sugar	pinch salt
3 egg yolks	¼ pint milk
3 oz. sultanas	few split almonds
1 lb. plain flour	icing sugar

* *To make babka you need a special tin, shaped like a fluted pudding basin. It is obtainable at shops or stores dealing with kitchen utensils for continental cooking.*

The name 'babka' means grandmother. There is also 'babas' which simply means woman or women. 'Babcczka' is the diminutive, meaning little woman. The name must have originated from the shape of the cake which resembles a woman's wide skirts.

Cream butter until soft and add sugar. Continue stirring and add egg yolks, one by one. Add washed, dried sultanas. Dissolve yeast in 1 tablespoon milk and stir until smooth. Allow to stand for 10 minutes and add salt, yeast mixture and, alternatively, flour and lukewarm milk to the rest of the dough. Beat very well with a wooden spoon until the dough blisters and looks smooth and glossy. Grease and flour a babka tin and put almonds into the fluted sides for decoration. Put in dough and let rise in a warm place until double in bulk (about 30–40 minutes).

Bake in a hot oven (425–450°F. or Gas mark 6–7) for 10 minutes, reduce to moderately hot (400°F. or Gas mark 5) and bake for 50 minutes. Let cool and sprinkle with icing sugar. This cake is eaten with tea or coffee.

Babka made with pumpkin *(Babka drożdżowa z dynią)*

10 oz. pumpkin	2 eggs
½ pint milk	3 oz. sugar
1 lb. flour	lemon rind
1 oz. yeast, fresh	4 oz. butter
icing sugar	

Peel pumpkin and remove seed. Grate on fine grater. Bring a quarter of the milk to the boil, add pumpkin and stirring well, simmer for 10 minutes. Sieve flour into bowl and make hollow in centre. Cream yeast with a quarter of the milk (lukewarm) and pour into the hollow. Mix well with a wooden spoon, cover the bowl with a teacloth and allow to rise in a warm place for 30 minutes.

Beat eggs, sugar and finely grated lemon peel, add cooled pumpkin mixture to this and mix well, either with a wooden spoon or with your hand. Melt butter and add to yeast mixture, work it well until it does not stick any more to spoon or hand. Fill a greased and floured babka tin half full, cover as before and allow to rise. When doubled in size, put into a hot oven (425–450°F. or Gas mark 6–7) and bake for about 45 minutes. Allow to cool in tin before turning it out. Sieve icing sugar over babka.

Crumble cake *(Ciasto z kruszonką)*

14 oz. flour	2 egg yolks
1 oz. fresh yeast	4 oz. sugar
½ pint milk	4 oz. butter
1 egg	orange peel

Sieve flour into a bowl and make a hollow in the centre. Cream yeast with 1 tablespoon lukewarm milk and pour into the hollow. Mix well, cover with a tea cloth and put into a warm place. Allow to rise. Meanwhile cream egg and yolks and sugar until foamy. Add to the risen flour mixture and beat with a wooden spoon or mix with hand. Add lukewarm, melted butter and finely grated orange peel and continue beating or mixing until the dough does not stick to the spoon or hand any more. Line a baking sheet with paper and make the edge about 2 inches high. Put the dough on this and spread with the blade of the knife.

Grate the crumble over the dough evenly and put in a warm place to rise. When dough is well risen, bake in hot oven (400°F. or Gas mark 6–7) for 35 minutes. Take out, sieve icing sugar over it and cut into 2-inch squares. Serve with tea or coffee.

For crumble:

4 oz. flour	2 oz. butter
2 oz. icing sugar	2 teaspoons cinnamon

Mix flour with sugar in a small bowl. Melt butter and add to this. Add cinnamon and make dough of these ingredients. It should be fairly hard as it must be grated on coarse grater.

Coffee cake with crumble top *(Drożdżowe ciasto z kruszonką)*

1 oz. fresh yeast
¼ pint milk
10 oz. flour
icing sugar

1½ oz. sugar
3 eggs
2 oz. butter

For topping:

5 oz. flour
4 oz. butter
3 oz. brown sugar

2 oz. ground almonds
1 teaspoon cinnamon

Cream yeast with 2 tablespoons lukewarm milk and 1 tablespoon flour. Let it stand in a warm place for 15 minutes. Cream sugar, eggs and butter until foamy, add the rest of the flour and lukewarm milk and yeast mixture and beat with a wooden spoon until smooth and glossy (about 15 minutes). Grease and flour baking sheet and make stiff edge of greaseproof paper about 1½–2 inches high. Fill dough into this (it should not be higher than ½ inch) and sprinkle crumble over it. To make crumble top put the ingredients on a pastry board and work with your fingers to achieve the consistency of very large breadcrumbs. Let rise in a warm place until double in height and bake in a hot oven (425–450° F. or Gas mark 6–7) for 45 minutes.

* To make crumble see previous recipe.

Cakes and pastries

Cakes and pastries are baked and eaten a lot in Poland. As in other European countries, women enjoy meeting for 'elevenses' at a café. In the afternoon, too, the café is a great meeting place. Certain groups of regular customers always sit at the same table and one knows that Mr. X. will be at this or that Kawiarnia - café with a group of friends. The cakes and pastries are of very good quality and there is a wide choice.

At home, however, women pride themselves on making their own favourite cake for their friends and families. Recipes are collected and exchanged and whenever one goes visiting one can be sure of finding some special cake or pastries on the table.

Albert biscuits *(Ciastka Albertki)*

7 oz. self-raising flour　　4 tablespoons top of milk
5½ oz. cornflour　　　　　　or cream
4 oz. butter　　　　　　　　5 oz. sugar
1 egg

Sieve the flours together. Cream butter till foamy, add whisked egg and cream and add sugar. Add flour little by little until you can make pastry with your hands and roll out to ¼-inch thickness. With a round pastry cutter or wine glass cut out rounds. Prick holes with a fork in each. Bake on a greased, floured baking sheet in a moderate oven (375° F. or Gas mark 4) for 25 minutes. The biscuits should not get brown.

Almond cookies *(Nugat zapiekany)*

8 oz. ground almonds　　3 egg whites
8 oz. sugar　　　　　　　redcurrant jelly
juice ½ lemon　　　　　　icing (see page 197, 198)

Mix ground almonds with sugar and lemon juice and add the stiffly beaten egg whites. Form 2 rolls 1½ inches in diameter and put on greased baking sheet. Bake in a slow oven (300° F. or Gas mark 2) for 15 to 20 minutes, when it should be half baked. Make a groove along the centre with the handle of a wooden spoon and bake for another 15 to 20 minutes to finish. Fill groove with jelly and put icing over it. Cut into thin slices before serving.

Apples in dressing gowns *(Jabłka w szlafrokach)*

8 oz. flour   2 egg yolks
6 oz. butter   cream

For filling:

1 lb. small apples   2 oz. vanilla sugar
6 oz. apricot jam   (see page 11)

Sieve flour on to pastry board. Cut butter into it, add egg yolks and a little cream and make into a soft pastry. The quantity of cream depends on the size of the egg yolks and it should only be added by spoonfuls.

Put pastry into bowl sprinkled with flour and let it stand in a cold place for 12 hours.

Peel and core apples. Roll out pastry to $\frac{1}{4}$ inch thickness, cut into squares of 4 inches and put half an apple in the centre. Put jam into the hollow where the core was removed and bring the 4 corners of the pastry to meet over the apple which should be completely covered. Put into a hot oven (425–450° F. or Gas mark 6-7) and bake for 20–25 minutes. The pastry should be golden and apples soft. Take out and sieve sugar over each piece.

Chocolate kisses *(Całusy z czekolady)*

4 oz. plain chocolate   1 egg white
5 oz. icing sugar

Melt chocolate. Put icing sugar on pastry board, add melted chocolate and mix with blade of knife. Add egg white and work it in until all is absorbed. Let it rest for at least 1 hour or longer. With your smallest pastry cutter cut out rounds not more than 1 inch in diameter, preferably less. Put on a greased baking sheet and bake in a slow oven (275° F. or Gas mark 1) for 1 hour. The kisses should be dry outside.

Chocolate slices (*Mazurek czekoladowy*)

3 oz. sugar	4 egg yolks
3 oz. butter	2 egg whites
3 oz. chocolate	2 oz. flour
2 oz. ground almonds	

For filling:

¼ pint coffee	2 oz. sugar
1 tablespoon milk	1 teaspoon cornflour
2 eggs	

Cream sugar with butter. Melt chocolate, cool and add together with ground almonds and yolks. Stir well for 10 minutes. Beat egg whites stiffly and fold in alternating with sieved flour.

Grease and flour baking sheet and spread mixture thinly. If necessary, spread half of another baking sheet. Bake in moderate oven (375° F. or Gas mark 4) for 20 minutes. *Meanwhile make filling.*

Add the milk to strong coffee and bring to boil. Stir egg yolks with cornflour and pour a little of the hot mixture over it, stirring well. Add to coffee and bring to boil, turn low immediately and simmer for 3 minutes. Let cool and add stiffly beaten egg whites. Cut pastry so that you have the same for top and bottom. Fill and cut into small squares.

Chocolate slices with apples (*Kruche ciasto czekoladowe z jabłkami*)

9 oz. flour	2 oz. chocolate
6½ oz. butter	2 oz. castor sugar
1 oz. ground hazel nuts	

For filling:

2 lb. apples	3 oz. sugar
2–3 tablespoons water	

170

Put flour on pastry board. Cut butter into it. Grind hazelnuts and chocolate and add as well as sugar. Knead dough. Divide in half. Grease and flour baking sheet. Roll out one half, put on to baking sheet and bake in a moderate oven (375° F. or Gas mark 4) for 12 to 15 minutes. The pastry should be lightly baked but not completely cooked.

Meanwhile peel apples, slice thinly and stew with water and sugar for 10 minutes. Drain if necessary. Put on pastry, roll out other half and cover top. Bake for 15 minutes. Cut into slices when cool.

Choux pastry for cream buns or éclairs *(Ptysie)*

½ pint water   7 oz. plain flour
4 oz. butter   4 eggs

Bring water with butter to the boil and add the sifted flour, stirring all the time until flour is absorbed and the mixture is smooth and leaves the sides of the saucepan, forming one lump. Remove from heat, cover and allow to stand for 1 hour. Now add eggs, one at a time. Grease a baking sheet. Using a forcing bag with a large pipe, make small, round shapes the size of a walnut or oblong ones for éclairs. Put into a moderately hot oven 400° F. or Gas mark 5) and bake for 30 minutes. Do not open oven door for the first 15 minutes as pastry will fall. When the pastry is a good colour, remove on to sieve to let it cool. When cold, slit open near the top but leave top connected in one place. Fill with whipped vanilla cream (see page 198). For éclairs cut open lengthways and fill.

If wanted, ice with chocolate icing (see page 197).

Christmas pastries *(Pierniki)*

5 eggs   vanilla essence
10 oz. sugar   pinch ground cloves
finely grated peel   pinch cinnamon
  1 lemon   5 oz. candied peel
finely grated peel   rice paper
  1 orange
10 oz. ground almonds
juice $\frac{1}{2}$ orange

For icing:

8 oz. sugar   lemon juice
1 egg white

For decorating:

1 oz. split almonds   glacé cherries

Whisk eggs with sugar until foamy. Add finely grated lemon and orange peel, almonds and orange juice. Add a few drops vanilla essence and spices. Chop peel finely and add. Line a baking sheet with foil to make edge all round about 1 inch high. Cover with rice paper and spread the mixture all over it to about $\frac{1}{2}$ inch thickness. Bake in a moderate oven (375° F. or Gas mark 4) for 30 minutes. Test with a wooden skewer (if it comes out clean, pastry is ready). Cut into squares while still warm. Let cool and ice.

To make icing: stir sugar, egg white and lemon juice until thick and white. Spread over each piece of pastry, unsig a palette knife. Put almond in centre and a small piece of cherry on each side.

Note: This pastry will keep well in a tin.

Easter pastry *(Mazurki)*

8 oz. plain flour	1 egg
pinch salt	2 tablespoons thin
4 oz. butter	cream
2 oz. sugar	

To decorate:

icing (see pages 197, 198)	angelica
glacé cherries	candied peel

Sieve flour and salt. Put on a pastry board and cut in butter and sugar. Beat egg with cream and add to mixture. Make dough and roll out till ⅓ inch thick. Put on greased and floured baking sheet or cake tin. Bake in a moderate oven (375° F. or Gas mark 4) for 30 minutes. Take from oven and cover quickly while still warm with one of the toppings in the following recipes. Bake according to topping instructions. When cool decorate with icing, glacé cherries, angelica or candied peel. Cut into pieces 1–2 inches.

Toppings for Mazurki

Mixed fruit

8 oz. sultanas	1 orange
8 oz. dates	4 oz. sugar
4 oz. nuts	2 eggs
1 lemon	

Chop fruit and nuts coarsely. Squeeze lemon and orange. Add juice, sugar and eggs to mixture. Stir well. Cover baked pastry with this mixture and return to a very moderate oven (300° F. or Gas mark 2) for 20 minutes.

Lemon topping

2 egg whites	8 oz. chopped almonds
4 oz. sugar	2 lemons

Whisk egg whites and sugar over hot water until thick. Remove from heat and add almonds, finely grated peel of 1 lemon and juice of both. Spread on baked pastry and put back into a very moderate oven (300°F. or Gas mark 2) for 10 minutes.

Vanilla topping

1 pint thin cream	3 oz. butter
14 oz. castor sugar	$\frac{1}{3}$ vanilla pod
3 egg yolks	

Whisk cream, sugar and egg yolks over boiling water until thickened. Remove from heat and add butter and scraped-out black inside of vanilla pod (see page 11). Put on baked pastry and cool.

Chrust and faworki

These are very popular pastries. *Faworki* means 'favours' and the shape of the pastry is reminiscent of a silk ribbon, given by a girl to a man at a dance. The word *chrust* means kindling wood, and the thin crisp pastry crackles like dry wood when eaten. The two pastries resemble each other and both should be eaten when fresh, as they lose their crispness very quickly.

Little favours *(Faworki)*

8 oz. flour	1 tablespoon rum,
2 oz. butter	whisky or brandy
1 egg white	fat for deep frying
3 egg yolks	icing sugar

Put first 5 ingredients into a bowl and knead. If necessary, add a little more flour (this depends on the size of the

174

eggs). Roll out on a floured pastry board until very thin and cut into 1½-inch wide strips. Now cut across diagonally, to make 'ribbon' about 4 inches long, with bias ends. Cut a slit 1 inch long near to one end and pull the other end through to form a loop.

Make the fat very hot in small saucepan and quickly fry each favour on both sides. Take out with a perforated spoon or fish slice, put on tissue or kitchen paper for a moment to remove surplus fat and sieve icing sugar over the favours. Serve straight away.

Chrust

1 lb. flour	1 oz. butter
sour cream	2½ oz. sugar
2 egg whites	fat for deep frying
4 egg yolks	icing sugar
1 teaspoon vinegar	

Work in the same way as for favours (see page 174). When rolled out very thinly, cut into strips 1 inch wide and 5 inches long. Cut 1-inch slit in centre, pull one end through this and continue as for favours.

Coffee kisses (Całusy kawowe)

3 egg whites	2 tablespoons water
7½ oz. sugar	
2 tablespoons instant coffee	

Whisk egg whites very stiffly. Bring 5 oz. sugar with instant coffee and water to the boil and cook until the liquid, running from a spoon, forms a drop at the end. Add this straight from heat to beaten whites, then add the remaining sugar and continue whisking until it is thick and cold. Put teaspoons of this on a greased baking sheet.

Bake in a cool oven (225–250° F. or Gas mark 0–½) for about 30 minutes or longer. Kisses should be dry underneath.

Decoration: (optional)

2 oz. chocolate   1 oz. vegetable fat

Melt both together and dribble across kisses in criss-cross pattern.

Family cookies *(Ciasteczka familijne)*

6 oz. butter   vanilla sugar
3 oz. castor sugar   (see page 11)
9 oz. flour

Put the first three ingredients on a pastry board and cut butter into flour and sugar with a knife. When crumbly, quickly make dough with your hands. Roll out thinly, cut into different shapes and bake on ungreased baking sheets.

Allow 15 minutes in a moderate oven (375° F. or Gas mark 4). Put on flat surface and while still warm, sieve sugar over cookies.

Honey cake *(Piernik)*

4 eggs   4 oz. chopped almonds
1 lb. sugar   4 oz. chopped candied
2 lb. honey   peel
1 tablespoon ginger $3\frac{1}{2}$ lb. flour
1 tablespoon cinnamon pinch bicarbonate
$\frac{1}{2}$ tablespoon ground   of potash
   cloves   1 tablespoon lukewarm
4 oz. raisins   water

The dough for this pastry should be made about 6 weeks in advance and baked when needed. As this recipe makes a large quantity but keeps well, it can be made in various shapes. They taste different, though made of the same dough, when baked in a bread tin or cut out. The part

176

which has been baked in a cake or bread tin can be left un-ced but the ones cut out as cookies should have chocolate icing (see page 197).

Whisk eggs and sugar till fluffy. Warm honey but do not allow it to become hot and slowly add to mixture. Add spices. Clean raisins and add as well as almonds and peel. Gradually add flour and bicarbonate, dissolved in water. Knead dough very well until it does not stick to fingers any more. Wrap it in a teacloth and keep in a cool place, but not the refrigerator.

When wanted, grease and flour cake or bread tins and fill half full. Bake in a moderate oven (375° F. or Gas mark 4) for 35 minutes. Let cool and turn out.

For cookies grease and flour baking sheets, roll out dough to about $\frac{1}{2}$ inch thickness and cut out in various shapes. Bake at same temperature but allow only 20 minutes. Store in tins.

Cinnamon slices (Kruche ciastka z cynamonem)

4 oz. flour	1 teaspoon powdered
4 oz. butter	cinnamon
2 oz. ground almonds	lemon peel
2 oz. castor sugar	

To decorate:
1 oz. split almonds

Sieve flour on to pastry board. Cut butter into it and add all the other ingredients, making short pastry. Roll out with rolling pin to less than $\frac{1}{4}$ inch thickness. With a pastry wheel cut into slices about $2 \times 1\frac{1}{2}$ inches. Put a split almond in the centre and bake in a moderate oven (375° F. or Gas mark 4) for 25 to 30 minutes. Allow to cool before removing.

Hussar kisses *(Całusy husara)*

| 6 oz. butter | 6 oz. flour |
| 3 oz. sugar | 3 oz. ground hazelnuts |

For topping:

    redcurrant jelly

Put the first 4 ingredients on pastry board. Blend with a knife. When crumbly, quickly make pastry with your fingers. Divide into 4 parts. Form a roll and cut off ½-inch long pieces. Press down to form small rounds. Make a hollow in centre of each with a thimble. Bake on greased, floured baking sheets in a moderate oven (375°F. or Gas mark 4) for 15–20 minutes, but half way through press hollows in the centre once more. Take out and let cool. Put a dot of jelly into the centre of each.

Jadzia's cookies *(Ciasteczka Jadzi)*

8 oz. butter	2 egg yolks
4 oz. soft brown sugar	4 oz. flour
4 oz. white sugar	4½ oz. oat flakes

For topping:

| 6 oz. chocolate | 2 oz. nuts or almonds |
| 2 oz. butter | |

Cream butter with both kinds of sugar. Add egg yolks, sieved flour and oats and stir well. Grease a 13-× 9-inch baking sheet. Spread mixture all over. Bake in moderate oven (375°F. or Gas mark 4) for 20 minutes. Let cool for 10 minutes. *To make topping:* melt chocolate and butter. Spread over pastry and sprinkle with coarsely chopped nuts. Cut into 1½-inch squares. This makes 48 cookies.

Macaroons *(Makaroniki)*

3 egg whites   6½ oz. castor sugar
5½ oz. hazel nuts

For decorating:

candied fruit

Whisk whites, adding ground hazel nuts and sugar alternately until mixture is thick. Grease a baking sheet and, using 2 teaspoons, form little mounds, at a distance from each other. Bake in slow oven (300°F. or Gas mark 2) for 15 to 20 minutes, after having pressed a small piece of candied peel on each macaroon.

Madeleines *(Magdalenki)*

6 egg yolks   1 tablespoon brandy
7 oz. sugar   (optional)
8 oz. flour   1 oz. roasted hazel nuts
4 oz. butter

Whisk egg yolks with sugar until light-coloured. Add flour by the spoonful and cooled melted butter. Lastly add brandy and whisk for 7 minutes. Butter cup cake forms and fill one quarter of each with mixture. Have coarsely chopped hazelnuts ready and sprinkle with these. Bake in a very moderate oven (300–350°F. or Gas mark 2–3) for 20 minutes.

These delicious cup cakes will keep fresh for several days.

Non plus ultra

As we knew this recipe under a Latin name, I give it in this name only. It is well deserved, as, when eaten fresh, it really is unsurpassed.

3 oz. sugar   9 oz. plain flour
6 oz. butter

For icing:

1 egg white   lemon juice
3 oz. icing sugar   jam

Cream sugar and butter till foamy. Add flour and mix. Knead dough quickly and put it into refrigerator for 1 hour. Roll out thinly and cut into fingers about 1 × 2 inches but do not separate.

Stir egg white with sugar until thick and white, gradually adding lemon juice drop by drop. Depending on the size of the egg white, you need more or less juice but even with a small white not more than the juice of ½ lemon will be required. Spread icing over fingers on pastry board and transfer the whole on a greased baking sheet. (If you can get white bees' wax for greasing, this is the best thing to use for this kind of pastry.)

Bake in a very moderate oven (300° F. or Gas mark 2) for 20 minutes. Let cool and sandwich two together with jam.

Shortbread stars *(Kruche gwiazdki)*

Though these stars can be used as biscuits the whole year round, they are particularly good to hang on the Christmas tree.

9 oz. flour   2 egg yolks
5 oz. butter   1 oz. granulated sugar
3 oz. castor sugar

Sieve flour on pastry board. Keep 1 tablespoon flour aside for rolling out. Cut butter into flour, add castor sugar, make a hollow in the centre of flour and put egg yolks into it. Make pastry with your hands. When smooth, divide in half as a smaller quantity is easier to work with. Sprinkle board with flour and roll pastry out to ⅛ inch thickness. Cut out stars in different sizes. If you are making them to hang on a tree, press hole in centre with a thimble. Sprinkle with granulated sugar and bake for 20–25 minutes in moderate oven (375° F. or Gas mark 4) on ungreased baking sheets. Let cool before removing.

Petits fours *(Rogaliki)*

7 oz. flour	3 oz. castor sugar
3 oz. grated chocolate	5 oz. butter
4 oz. almonds	2 egg yolks

For decorating:

1 oz. almonds	drop green edible colour

For icing:

3 oz. chocolate	½ oz. butter

Put flour and chocolate on pastry board. Grind unpeeled almonds and add the last 3 ingredients. Cut butter and egg yolks into pastry and when blended quickly work through with your fingers to make pastry. Divide into 6 parts. Let rest for 30 minutes. With the palm of your hand roll pastry into a sausage the thickness of your finger. Cut off a small piece, roll into a 2-inch length about ½ inch thick. Bring the ends towards you to form a small crescent. Continue like this until all parts are used up. Put on ungreased baking sheets and bake in a moderate oven (375° F. or Gas mark 4) for 25 minutes. Meanwhile prepare icing and decoration. Blanch almonds and chop finely when peeled. Dye almonds green and let dry. Melt chocolate and add butter. Dip both ends of crescents in this and sprinkle almonds over them.

Suet crescents (*Rogaliki na łoju*)

7 oz. flour
2 oz. lard
2 oz. sugar
icing sugar

⅛ pint and 1 tablespoon white wine
8 oz. suet

For filling:

jam filling
(see page 207)

Put flour, lard and sugar on a pastry board and make a hollow in the centre. Put wine into this and work all together to make a soft dough. Let stand for 30 minutes. Divide suet in 4 parts. Roll out dough and put one part of suet in centre. Fold over and roll out. Put the second part on to it and repeat. When all 4 parts are used up, allow dough to rest in cold place for 1 hour.

Roll out thinly and with a knife, dipped into hot water, cut out 3-inch squares. Put filling in centre, fold over to form triangle and turn over corners.

Bake in very hot oven (475–500°F. or Gas mark 8–9) for 15–20 minutes. Crescents should be golden. Sieve icing sugar over tops.

Tea cake (*Sucharki*)

2 eggs
5 oz. vanilla sugar
(see page 11)

4 oz. flour
icing sugar

Stir all ingredients together until you have a thick batter. Grease and flour a baking sheet and divide the mixture in half. Make 2 rolls and mark a groove in the centre with the handle of a wooden spoon. Bake in a slow oven (275°–300°F. or Gas mark 1-2) for 30 minutes. Sprinkle with icing sugar while still warm. Slice.

Variation: If wanted, the sliced tea cake can be baked again so that each slice is golden-coloured and very crisp and dry.

182

Quick tea pastries *(Szybkie ciasteczka do herbaty)*

These pastries can be made at the last moment before they are needed. They are best eaten fresh, and slightly warm.

4 oz. flour	jam for filling
4 oz. butter	icing sugar
4 oz. curd cheese	

Mix the first three ingredients together with a knife. Quickly work through with your hands. Roll out pastry about ¼ inch thick. With a pastry wheel cut into squares of 2 inches. Put ½ teaspoon jam in centre and fold over one corner on top of the other. Press down edges to seal in jam. Bake in a hot oven (425° F. or Gas mark 6) for 15–20 minutes. Put on a dish and sieve sugar over the pastries.

Warsaw fingers *(Paluszki warszawskie)*

5 oz. ground almonds	1 egg white
5 oz. icing sugar	

For icing:

4 oz. icing sugar	1 egg white
juice ½ lemon	

Put almonds and sugar on pastry board. Make a well in the centre and put in the egg white. Mix together with knife then continue to work into dough with fingers. If necessary sprinkle a little icing sugar on board to prevent sticking. Roll out thinly into a strip 3 inches wide. Cut into 1-inch lengths.

Make icing by stirring all 3 ingredients together until the mixture is thick and white (about 15 minutes). Ice fingers and put on a baking sheet greased preferably with bees-wax (see page 11). Bake in a very slow oven (275° F. or Gas mark 1) for 15–20 minutes. The icing should harden but not colour. Allow to cool and remove carefully.

Vanilla crescents *(Rogaliki waniliowe)*

4 oz. hazelnuts   10 oz. flour
4 oz. castor sugar   8 oz. butter

For covering:

4 oz. vanilla sugar
(see page 11)

Roast hazelnuts in moderate oven (375° F. or Gas mark 4) until the skins burst. Take out and rub in a cloth to remove skins as much as possible. Grind. Mix with sugar and flour and put on a pastry board. Using knife, cut in butter until crumbly, then work with hands. Divide in half. Make a roll the thickness of your little finger. Cut off 2-inch long pieces, bend ends to form a crescent and put on an ungreased baking sheet. Bake in a moderate oven (375° F. or Gas mark 4) for 15–20 minutes. It is necessary to take out the crescents as they are getting ready, as oven temperature is not the same all over baking sheet. Using blade of knife, take out crescents and immediately put into vanilla sugar to coat them all round. Take out carefully as they are very brittle when fresh.

Gâteaux

Gâteaux and rich pastries are part of the Polish cooking tradition. We know that at the wedding of one of the kings of Poland the royal table was adorned with two pyramidal wedding cakes, each ten feet high, gilded and painted in various colours, with allegorical figures and inscriptions befitting the celebration. Nowadays, though, cakes are much less decorated than in England. There are no particular wedding cakes or Christmas cakes and only Easter has the traditional mazurky. Yet, as far as richness is concerned, Polish cakes have richer ingredients and many recipes use no flour but ground nuts instead. Butter cream, either with coffee, chocolate or nuts, is often used for filling and covering a gâteau, although thick cream, to which other ingredients may have been added, is also popular.

Ania's strawberry tart *(Tort truskawkowy Ani)*

5½ oz. butter	1½ oz. sugar
5½ oz. plain flour	1 teaspoon water

For topping:

4 tablespoons raspberry jelly	½ teaspoon cornflour
	8 oz. strawberries

Cut butter into small pieces on pastry board. Sieve flour and add sugar and water to it. Work this into butter for pastry. Let rest in a cold place for at least 30 minutes. Roll out and line 9-inch flan or pie dish. Bake in a moderate oven (350°F. or Gas mark 3) for 20 to 25 minutes. It should be golden coloured. Take out and let cool but leave it in the dish, as this pastry is very rich and crumbly.

Bring jelly with cornflour to the boil and simmer for a few minutes till clear. Put strawberries on to the pastry (if very large ones are used, halve them) and pour the jelly over it. Let get cold and serve with cream.

Puff pastry *(Ciasto francuskie)*

Main dough:

8 oz. flour	½ tablespoon vinegar
1 egg yolk	cold water

Butter dough:

10 oz. butter	2 oz. flour

Make main dough by sieving flour into bowl and adding the other ingredients. Water must be added by the spoonful and a palette knife should be used to cut ingredients into flour. When enough liquid has been absorbed to make smooth pastry, turn it out on a pastry board and knead until smooth and not too stiff. Put in a cold place for 15 minutes. *Meanwhile make butter dough:* put butter into a teacloth or loosely woven cloth and squeeze out as much moisture as possible. Sieve flour and add butter. Work into a smooth dough. Roll out the main dough into an oblong shape. Put the butter dough in the centre, then fold ends over it, making a fold of three. Press the edges together and turn the dough so that the folded edge is at side. Press several times with a rolling pin and put the pastry into the refrigerator for 15 minutes. Roll out after that time into a strip of about 15 inches length, keeping the edges as straight as possible. Fold in three again, turn the fold to the side and press lightly with a rolling pin. Let it rest in the refrigerator again. Repeat these turns twice more. Put into a cloth in the icebox for several hours before finally using it.

Cream slices *(Napoleonki)*

puff pastry (see page 186) ½ pint thick cream
4 tablespoons jam 4 oz. icing sugar

After having worked the pastry as directed on page 186, divide into 2 halves, roll out to ½ inch thickness and cut into slices 1½ × 3 inches. Bake in a very hot oven 475°–500° F. or Gas mark 8–9) for 12 minutes. Leave to cool. Spread half the slices with jam and with stiffly whipped cream, to which 3 oz. sugar has been added. Put other slices on top and sieve the rest of the icing sugar over the finished slices.

French pastry with vanilla cream *(Ciasta francuskie z kremem)*

puff pastry (see page 186)

For filling:

1 pint milk	1 oz. cornflour
4 egg yolks	
4 oz. vanilla sugar	
(see page 11)	

For top:

1 oz. icing sugar

Make pastry. Roll out to $\frac{3}{8}$ inch thickness, divide in halves and bake each half on an ungreased baking sheet in a hot oven (425°–450° F. or Gas mark 6–7) for 15 minutes. Take out and let cool. For filling bring $\frac{1}{2}$ pint mink to boil, stir yolks and sugar till foamy and cream cornflour with the other $\frac{1}{2}$ pint milk. Pour boiling milk over cold milk mixture, return to heat and, stirring constantly, bring to the boil again. Add the egg mixture, being careful not to boil it any more, only allowing it to thicken. Put the saucepan into cold water and continue stirring. Take pastry and spread cooled cream over one half, then cover with second half. With a long sharp knife cut into slices 2 inches wide and 3 inches long. Sieve sugar over finished slices.

Poppyseed cake *(Makowiec)*

4 oz. poppyseed*	3 oz. candied peel
3 eggs	3 oz. sultanas
4 oz. sugar	3 oz. dates
4 oz. ground walnuts or	3 oz. self-raising flour
hazel nuts	chocolate icing
	(see page 197)

* *Poppyseed can be bought in most continental food shops. The seed should be ground, and a special mill is necessary*

for this. If it is not available already ground at the shop, scald seed three times, always pouring off water when it has cooled. Pass seed twice through mincer using smallest disc.

Beat eggs and add sugar, nuts and chopped fruit. Sieve flour twice and add this and poppyseed to mixture. Grease and flour an 8-inch cake tin and bake the cake in a moderate oven (375° F. or Gas Mark 4) for 45 minutes. Ice next day with chocolate icing.

Semi-French pastry with fruit *(Ciastka pół-francuskie z masą owocową)*

8 oz. flour	8 oz. curd cheese
8 oz. butter	

For topping:

3 egg whites	8 oz. icing sugar
8 oz. strawberries or	juice 1 lemon
raspberries	

Sieve flour. Cut in butter and work into flour. Pass cheese through sieve and quickly work it into the flour mixture. Roll out thinly (about ¼ inch) and cut out rounds of about 2 inches or more. Put on an ungreased baking sheet and bake in a moderately hot oven 400° F. or Gas mark 5) for 20 minutes.

Whisk egg whites till very stiff. Wash and dry fruit. Add sugar, spoon by spoon, to whites, continuing whisking. When the mixture is very stiff, add berries by the spoonful, stirring them in. Add lemon juice in small quantities. It may not be necessary to use up all the lemon juice, depending on the sourness of the fruit. When all is thickened sufficiently, pipe pyramids of the mixture on to each cooled pastry disc.

Pischinger cake *(Tort Pischinger)*

This uncooked cake is quick to prepare. Pischinger was the name of the firm who introduced the round wafers, bought by the packet, for this particular cake. Though the wafers are now manufactured by other firms also, the name of the cake remains. Another kind of wafer, particularly good for this cake, though more expensive, are Karlsbad Oblaten, imported from Czechoslovakia. (Karlsbad is a spa with excellent water.) It is advisable to crisp the wafers in a hot oven before using.

1 packet* round wafers 6 oz. plain chocolate
   about 9 inches in 2 oz. ground roasted
   diameter   hazelnuts
8 oz. butter 1 egg yolk
   (preferably unsalted)

* *Each packet contains several wafers.*

Cream butter and add cooled, melted chocolate. If you like, add a little castor sugar, but as chocolate is rather sweet, this is not really necessary. Add nuts and egg yolk and stir till smooth and glossy.

Spread wafer with this, then put next on top and continue until all the wafers are used up, leaving top uncovered. Put a bread board on top and weigh down with tins. Put the cake into a cold place for 2 hours. The top can be left plain or iced with chocolate icing (see page 197). Cut with a sharp knife.

Layer cake *(Przekładaniec)*

8 oz. suet or butter
10 oz. plain flour
6 oz. castor sugar
2 egg yolks

1 tablespoon rum
1 oz. icing sugar

For filling:

1. 2 large cooking apples
   2 oz. sugar
2. 2 oz. ground almonds
   1 oz. sugar
3. 3 tablespoons strawberry
   jam
4. 2 oz. bar chocolate

Rub fat into flour as for short crust pastry. Add sugar, egg yolks and rum to make dough. Divide into five equal parts. Draw five circles, each 8 inches in diameter, on separate pieces of greaseproof paper. Roll out dough into five parts to fit each circle. Bake on paper in a very moderate oven (300° F. |or Gas mark 2) for 15–20 minutes. Allow to cool on paper, then remove. Meanwhile make the fillings:

1. Peel apples and slice thinly. Add sugar and cook till soft. Allow to cool.
2. Add sugar to almonds and mix well.
3. Spread jam.
4. Melt chocolate and spread.

Put one filling between each layer, covering with the fifth layer. Sprinkle the top with icing sugar.

Aunt Caroline's gâteau *(Tort cioci Karoliny)*

4 eggs	4 oz. almonds
4 oz. sugar	

For filling and topping:

2 eggs	3 oz. castor sugar
4 oz. butter, preferably unsalted	3 tablespoons water

Beat eggs with sugar until foamy. Keep 12 almonds and grind the rest (unpeeled) and add to eggs. Grease and flour an 8-inch cake tin and put the mixture in. Bake in a moderate oven (375° F. or Gas mark 4) for about 45 minutes, testing it with a wooden skewer which should come out dry when pushed into the cake. Allow to cool, turn out and halve.

Cream egg yolks and butter until fluffy. Bring sugar and water to the boil and simmer until it begins to thicken slightly. Let cool and add to butter cream. Whisk egg whites very stiffly and fold in. Fill cake with this and cover top and sides. Blanch the 12 almonds, split and decorate the cake with them. Keep in the refrigerator for a few hours before serving.

Meringue flan *(Tort kruchy z pianką)*

4 oz. flour	2 oz. castor sugar
3 oz. butter	3 egg yolks

For topping:

3 egg whites	3 tablespoons jam
3 oz. icing sugar	
1 packet Vanillin or	
¾ oz. vanilla sugar	

Sieve flour on to pastry board. Cut butter into flour, add sugar and egg yolks and make pastry with your hands. If it is sticky, put it into cold place for an hour and work it through after that. Line an 8-inch cake

and work it through after that. Line an 8-inch cake tin with pastry and make edge. Bake in a hot oven (425°–450°F. or Gas mark 6–7) for 15–20 minutes. The pastry should be golden coloured. Take out but leave pastry in tin. Whisk egg whites very stiffly and gradually whisk sugar into whites. Whisk for 10 more minutes, having added vanilla sugar also. Spread pastry with jam and put meringue on top. Return to moderate heat (375°F. or Gas mark 4) and bake for about 15 minutes. The meringue should be slightly coloured and hardened. Take out and loosen sides by going around the edges with a palette knife. Serve on the same day, as meringue collapses.

Kościuszko cake (Tort Kościuszko)

This cake is named after a Polish national hero. Why, nobody knows. Perhaps he liked it.

4 eggs	4 oz. ground almonds
4 oz. sugar	4 oz. chocolate

For topping:

½ pint thick cream	2 tablespoons rum or brandy

For icing:

4 oz. chocolate	1 teaspoon butter
1 tablespoon black coffee	

Whisk egg yolks with sugar until foamy. Fold in almonds and melted, cooled chocolate. Grease an 8-inch cake tin and bake cake in a moderate oven (375°F. or Gas mark 4) for 50–60 minutes. Allow to cool, turn out and leave to stand till next day.

Cut off the top of the cake (about a quarter of its thickness) and crumble it up finely. Beat the cream until

193

stiff, add crumbs and rum or brandy and cover cake with this. Make icing by melting chocolate with coffee in a double saucepan. When dissolved, add butter and quickly cover cream topping with this. Allow to stand in a cold place for 2 hours before serving.

Cheese cake *(Sernik)*

For short pastry:

8 oz. plain flour	2 egg yolks
4 oz. butter	1 tablespoon cold water

For filling:

1½ lb. curd cheese	6 oz. butter
10 oz. castor sugar	grated lemon peel
4 eggs	3 oz. fine semolina

Put flour on pastry board, cut butter into it and add egg yolks and water. While using knife to begin with, knead through when ingredients are blended. Roll out and put aside one-third of the dough. Line a 9-inch cake tin, prick dough in several places and bake for 20 minutes in a moderate oven (375° F. or Gas mark 4).

For filling: rub cheese through sieve. Cream sugar, egg yolks, butter and lemon peel (use the yellow part only, finely grated). Beat egg whites until very stiff and fold in, alternating with semolina. Take cake bottom from oven and put cheese mixture over it. Make a trellis with the rest of the dough, rolling it out and cutting it into narrow strips with a pastry wheel or knife. Bake in a moderate oven (375° F. or Gas mark 4) for 45 minutes.

Variation: Bake filling without base and trellis.

The best gâteau *(Tort wyborowy)*

8 oz. butter	4 oz. ground almonds
8 oz. plain flour	3 oz. icing sugar

For filling:

5 oz. ground hazelnuts	$\frac{1}{4}$ pint thick cream
or walnuts	3 oz. icing sugar

For topping:

chocolate icing
(see page 197)

Cut butter into flour, almonds and sugar on pastry board and knead into dough with your fingertips. Divide in to four equal parts and roll out into rounds, each 8 inches in diameter. If you have not got suitable tins, draw circles on greaseproof paper and bake on this. Remove when cold.

Bake in a very slow oven (250°F. or Gas mark $\frac{1}{2}$) for 15 minutes. Allow to cool.

For filling:

Add nuts to stiffly beaten cream and sugar and fill gâteau. Cover with icing.

This, as well as many others in this book, is a family recipe, hence the name.

Uncooked Easter pudding *(Pascha)*

10–12 Servings

2 lb. curd cheese	3 oz. chopped almonds
5 egg yolks	3 oz. sultanas
10 oz. castor sugar	½ vanilla pod
½ pint thick cream	
6 oz. butter, preferably unsalted	

For decorating:

angelica	glacé cherries

You will also need a new flowerpot 6–7 inches in diameter, previously soaked for 24 hours, and a piece of muslin for lining the pot.

Rub cheese through sieve. Cream yolks and sugar and add half the quantity of cream. Heat this slowly but do not allow to boil. Cream butter and add this and cheese to the cooled mixture. Add almonds and sultanas. Split vanilla pod in half lengthways, scrape out black inside and add this to the mixture (see page 11 for use of vanilla pod).

Line the flowerpot with muslin, leaving enough material to cover the top when filled. Fill the pot with the mixture and cover with muslin. Put a plate on top of the mixture and weigh it down with weights or a heavy tin. Hang up pot, being careful to keep it straight, or put it into a bowl where it will not touch the bottom so that liquid can escape through the hole in bottom of pot. Keep in cool place for 1 day. Turn out carefully, remove muslin, whisk the other half of the cream and, using a forcing bag, decorate the sides of the pudding with this as well as glacé cherries and small sprigs of angelica.

Quick icing *(Szybki lukier)*

This icing is particularly good for writing on other icing for a birthday cake or other decoration. It dries very quickly.

2 oz. icing sugar	2 teaspoons egg white

Stir both together and test to see if a drop of the mixture, put on the edge of a saucer, hardens. Fill an icing bag and write on dry icing on cake. For different colouring use a drop of cochineal, saffron or cocoa.

Sugar icing *(Lukier)*

8 oz. lump sugar	$\frac{1}{4}$ pint water

Bring sugar and water to the boil and simmer until it thickens. To test if it is the right degree of thickening, let it drop from spoon and blow at it when it should form a thread.

Remove from heat and put into a bowl. With a wooden spoon stir until the icing turns white. For flavouring add lemon or orange juice or 1 tablespoon instant coffee dissolved in 2 tablespoons boiling water.

Chocolate icing *(Lukier czekoladowy)*

12 lumps sugar	4 oz. plain chocolate
2 tablespoons water	$\frac{1}{2}$ oz. butter

Simmer sugar in water for a few minutes until it begins to thicken slightly. At the same time melt chocolate either over a pan of boiling water or in a warm oven. Add syrup gradually to chocolate, stirring all the time until smooth and glossy; then add butter, stirring it in. Use straight away as this icing hardens very quickly.

White icing *(Biały lukier)*

This quantity will ice a medium-sized cake.

5 oz. icing sugar
2 teaspoons lemon
juice

2 tablespoons orange
juice
1–2 tablespoons water

Rub sugar through sieve. Strain fruit juices. Stir all together until the icing is smooth and begins to thicken. Pour it over the cake and use a palette knife to spread the icing down over the sides. Let it dry in a warm but not hot place.

Variation: Use 2 tablespoons of strong coffee instead of fruit juices.

Vanilla cream for filling and icing cakes *(Krem waniliowy do tortów)*

The quantity given below is sufficient for filling an 8–9 inch cake. If wanted also for covering, double the quantity.

3 oz. unsalted butter
1½ oz. icing sugar
½ packet Vanillin or
1 tablespoon icing sugar
with scraped-out inside
of ¼ vanilla pod (see
page 11)

1 egg yolk
1 teaspoon brandy or
rum

Cream butter. Sieve sugar and gradually add all the ingredients to butter, stirring until smooth.

Confectionery

In Poland chocolates are excellent, often flavoured with spirits, and less figure-conscious women can enjoy a wide variety of confectionery. The ambitious housewife makes her own. If possible, bitter chocolate is preferable to plain for home-made confectionery. Most town-dwellers have relatives in the country and therefore various kinds of nuts can often be had for the asking, or better still, collected in the autumn. Bee-keeping, too, is widely spread and honey, a necessary ingredient for some confectionary, is easily obtained.

Apricot delights *(Rozkosz z moreli)*

8 oz. dried apricots   2 oz. candied orange
water
8 oz. sugar   peel
4 oz. almonds, chopped   sugar for coating

Soak apricots overnight, allowing enough water just to cover them. Boil together with sugar (the water should be absorbed by apricots when soaking) until thick. Add almonds and chopped peel. Form a sausage about $1\frac{1}{2}$ inches thick and roll in sugar. When completely dry, slice thinly.

Prune sausage *(Kiełbasa ze śliwek)*

1 lb. prunes   4 oz. sultanas
6 oz. chopped almonds   6 oz. sugar
3 oz. candied peel   peel 1 lemon
4 oz. dried figs   sugar to coat

Wash prunes, bring to the boil just covered with water and simmer, covered, for 20 minutes or until soft. Strain, stone and chop finely. Add all the other ingredients, being careful to chop fruit finely. Only the yellow part of lemon peel is used and this, too, must be cut very small. Put all together into a thick saucepan (preferably heavy iron) and cook, stirring all the time, for 10 minutes.

Sprinkle pastry board with sugar, put cooled mixture on to this and form a sausage about 1 inch in diameter. Put this on greaseproof paper and let it lie for 6–8 days. Slice thinly and put each slice in a paper cup.

Nougat *(Nugat)*

5 egg whites   2 tablespoons cornflour
8 oz. clear honey   10 oz. nuts
1 lb. icing sugar

Whisk egg whites very stiffly. Warm honey slightly. Add sugar to egg whites and continue beating. Add honey and cornflour and beat for 10 minutes with a wooden spoon. Chop nuts coarsely and add to mixture. Put mixture into a heavy saucepan (preferably an iron one) and place on a very low gas flame or hotplate, stirring all the time to prevent it from getting burnt. Keep it like this for 20 minutes or until it starts thickening. Pour on to a sheet of rice paper and cover with a second sheet. Straighten the sides with the blade of a knife and even the top by passing rolling pin over it lightly. When cool cut quickly with a hot knife (dipped into boiling water). The slices should be about 1 inch wide and 2 inches long.

Nut crunch *(Makagigi)*

8 oz. honey   2 tablespoons dried
4 oz. sugar   breadcrumbs
10 oz. nuts

Cook honey and sugar, stirring all the time, until it is all dissolved and has turned a light caramel colour. Quickly add coarsely chopped nuts (preferably walnuts) and continue stirring. At the last moment add breadcrumbs and mix. Have a wet wooden board ready on which you pour the mixture and with a wet rolling pin roll out to the thickness of your little finger (a little over $\frac{1}{4}$ inch). Cut quickly into $1\frac{1}{2}$-inch squares and smooth the surface with the blade of a knife. When storing, put greaseproof paper between layers, as it would otherwise stick together.

Truffles *(Trufle czekoladowe)*

8 oz. chocolate	2 egg yolks
4 oz. butter	1½ oz. cocoa to coat
¼ pint thick cream	

Melt chocolate and add, slightly cooled, to creamed butter. Add the other ingredients and stir well until the mixture is firm and glossy.

Put the cocoa into a small, deep dish (a cereal or fruit plate will do). Form small balls a little larger than hazelnut, and coat with cocoa, putting each ball into plate separately, shaking the plate. Put each truffle into a paper cup.

Honey truffles *(Trufle z miodu)*

3 tablespoons honey	1 teaspoon rum or
6 oz. roasted hazel nuts	brandy
orange and lemon peel	pinch cinnamon
	cocoa for coating

Bring honey with roasted and coarsely chopped nuts to boil. Add peel (yellow parts only) cut into very thin small slivers, stir and simmer for 15–20 minutes. Add rum and cinnamon. Let mixture cool. Put cocoa into a small bowl. Form little balls, the size of nut, put each singly into the cocoa and shake the bowl to coat each truffle. When finished, put each into a paper cup.

Grillage almonds *(Migdałki w cukrze)*

8 oz. almonds   3 tablespoons water
8 oz. lump sugar   ¼ vanilla pod

Skin almonds. Bring sugar with water and vanilla pod to the boil and simmer for 10–12 minutes. The syrup should be quite thick. Remove vanilla and add almonds to syrup. Continue cooking, stirring all the time. The sugar will caramelize and the almonds will have a golden brown coating. Grease baking sheet well with oil and spread the almonds out on this, allowing them to dry. When dry, take off. As almonds remain sticky when stored, put greaseproof paper between the layers of almonds in tin or box.

Nut balls *(Trufle orzechowe)*

4 oz. walnuts   2 tablespoons water
4 oz. sugar   2 oz. chocolate

For filling:
1 hard-boiled egg yolk   zhite icing
2 oz. icing sugar   (see page 198)*
1 dessertspoon rum   nuts for decoration

* *if icing in various colours is wanted, add a drop of edible colouring to part of it.*

Grind nuts. Bring sugar and water to the boil and simmer until it begins to thicken. Add to nuts and grated chocolate. *Prepare filling:* pass egg yolk through sieve and add to sieved sugar and rum. Take a little of the nut mixture, press it flat and put a little filling on it. Form a small ball. When all the balls are shaped, dip into icing and press a small piece of nut into this. Allow to dry and put each into a paper cup.

Chestnut sausage *(Kiełbasa z kasztanów)*

1 8-oz. can unsweetened chestnut purée	1 tablespoon rum
	2 oz. candied fruit
3 oz. butter	chocolate icing
3 oz. icing sugar	(see page 197)

Cream chestnut purée with butter and gradually add the other ingredients, except the icing. Form into a 1-inch thick sausage and let it stand in a cold place overnight. Next day cover with chocolate icing. Slice thinly.

Chocolate salami *(Salami z czekolady)*

Salami is a dry kind of sausage, eaten in most continental countries. This confectionery looks a little like it as the white pieces of almonds or nuts resemble the bits of fat in the real salami.

8 oz. plain chocolate	1 tablespoon instant coffee
8 oz. almonds or nuts	
2 oz. candied peel	5 tablespoons water
8 oz. sugar	sugar to coat

Grate chocolate. Skin almonds or roast hazel nuts and grate half of these. Chop the other half and add all together with peel to chocolate. Bring sugar with coffee, dissolved in boiling water, to boil and simmer until it begins to thicken but does not change colour. Pour hot over chocolate mixture and stir until well mixed. Sprinkle sugar on pastry board, put mixture on this and form a sausage about 1 inch in diameter. Put on greaseproof paper for 2 days before slicing it thinly. Put each slice in a paper cup.

Jams and confiture

Jam, as we know it, is called marmolada in Poland and this is prepared roughly in the same way as in most other countries. Konfitura, on the other hand, is a completely different thing, though it also consists of fruit and sugar. It needs a lot of preparation and is not eaten on bread and butter, but served on very small special dishes, either crystal or porcelain, and is taken by the spoon with tea. Small spoons, the size of egg spoons, are used for eating konfitura. It can be made of all sorts of fruits, cherries sweet and sour, and others. The fruit should remain whole and the juice is slightly thinner than in jam. Both stones and pips are removed which is not easy when dealing with redcurrants. A pin is used for this operation and the skin of the berry must not be damaged more than is essential. One needs a lot of time to make this konfitura — a whole morning's work will only produce one jar. But as with other works of art, it cannot be hurried. Gooseberries are quicker to prepare and the round end of a new hairpin will get the pips out comparatively easily.

Sweet and sour cherries are stoned but must not be squashed. To keep fruit firm it is dipped in alcohol for a moment. In Poland, 75% alcohol obtainable anywhere is used for this purpose but brandy, whisky or wódka can be used instead.

To make konfitura:

1. Wash fruit. Berries are best rinsed in a strainer. Dry and remove stalks, stones or pips.
2. Prepare syrup as follows: to 2 lb. sugar bring ½ pint water to the boil. Simmer for 15 minutes. Dip fruit in alcohol (optional).
3. Carefully add fruit to syrup and simmer for 30 minutes. Do not stir but shake pan from time to time. Skim off impurities.
4. Let stand until next day. Leave fruit in syrup, bring to the boil and simmer for 15 minutes, or until the fruit begins to look glassy.
5. Use small jars for storing. Fill with cool konfitura, cover with a waxed disc then with celophane. Keep in a cool dry place.

Jam *(Dżem)*

To each lb. fruit use 8–12 oz. sugar. All kinds of fruit
are suitable for jam. In contrast to confiture, here the
fruit is more or less pulped. To set jam, it is advisable
to add fruit with a high pectin content or lemon juice.
Also jam can be made of less perfect fruit.

1. Wash fruit and cut away blemished parts. Remove
   stones if possible. Stalks must be removed.
2. If much has been removed, weigh again. Allow ¼ pint
   water per lb. of fruit, ½ pint for hard fruit such as
   gooseberries, blackcurrants etc. Simmer until soft.
3. Add sugar and boil fast. Stir frequently, remove scum
   as it rises and test after about 20 minutes.
4. If a drop of liquid sets on a saucer, remove from heat
   and fill jars. Put spoon into jar to avoid cracking when
   filling in hot jam. Cover with a cellophane disc and
   cover jars with greaseproof paper or cellophane. Keep
   in a cool, dry place.

Plum jam for filling flans and tarts *(Marmolada ze
śliwek do tortow lub ciastek)*

8 lb. ripe plums	¼ pint wine vinegar
4 lb. sugar	2 cinnamon sticks

Wash plums and remove stones. Bring sugar with vinegar
to the boil and add plums and cinnamon. Stir frequently
and cook until plums are mashed. Keep in a stone jar
for 1–2 weeks. When the jam becomes thinner after
that time, bring to the boil again and simmer for 15 minutes. Remove cinnamon. Put into jars, cover with a disc
of greaseproof paper soaked in alcohol such as whisky
or brandy, cover jar and tie up. Keep in a cool place.

Good plum jam for cake fillings (Dobra marmolada ze śliwek do tortów)

5 lb. plums
1½ lb. sugar

5 tablespoons wine vinegar
½ cinnamon stick

The best plums for this recipe are the dark, oblong plums called Switchen. (This is a name derived from its Austrian name, Zwetschken.)

Pour boiling water over plums and remove skins. If this is not possible, put them into boiling water for 2 or 3 minutes, strain and remove skin. Take out stones. Bring sugar and vinegar to the boil, remove scum and add cinnamon and plums. Simmer for 20 to 30 minutes until there is an even, thickish mixture but stir frequently as this is apt to catch. Fill into large jar (preferably earthenware), cover lightly and let it stand for 1 or 2 weeks, or until it gets thinner. Then bring to the boil again and simmer for 10 to 15 minutes. After that, put into jars and cover with cellophane. Keep in a cool, dry place.

Peach confiture (Konfitura z brzoskwiń)

2 lb. ripe peaches

2 lb. sugar

Pour boiling water over peaches and remove skin. Drain. Cut in halves and take out stones. Put halves in bowl so that cut side is upwards and sprinkle with sugar. Do this layer by layer and let stand until the next day.

Put all together into a preserving pan, bring to the boil and immediately turn heat low and simmer for 20 minutes. Take out peach halves, put into jars and bring syrup again to the boil. Simmer until it shows signs of thickening, but do not allow it to crystallize. Remove immediately, let it cool and pour over peaches. Cover lightly. After 8–10 days pour off syrup and simmer it again for 10–15 minutes. When cool, pour over peaches and cover with cellophane. Keep in a cool, dry place.

Lemon confiture *(Konfitura z cytryn)*

4 medium-sized lemons   ½ pint water for syrup
2½ lb. sugar

Wash lemons, peel very thinly and keep peel. Put this as well as lemons, cut into quarters, into slightly salted water, enough to cover lemons. After 24 hours pour off water, renew, again salt slightly and put in lemons for another 24 hours. Repeat this changing of the water for the next 3 days. By then it should not taste bitter any longer. Put into fresh cold water and bring to the boil. Simmer for 30 minutes. Strain and discard water. Make syrup (see page 206) and add finely cut peel to this. With a small spoon take out all the flesh of the lemon and discard the skin between sections as well as the outer skin. Put into boiling syrup and simmer for 15 minutes. Next day take out fruit, bring syrup to boil and put fruit back. Remove immediately from heat. Strain syrup again or remove fruit, bring the syrup to the boil and pour over fruit. Repeat this once or twice more on following days and then put all together in small jars and cover with cellophane.

Spiced cherry jam *(Marmolada z czereśni z korzeniami)*

4 lb. black ripe cherries   4 cloves
1½ lb. sugar   ¼ pint water
½ cinnamon stick

Wash and stalk cherries. Remove stones. Bring sugar, spices and water to the boil and allow to simmer until it begins to thicken. Add cherries and boil for 25–30 minutes. Put in a stone jar or china bowl and cover lightly. After 5 or 6 days bring to the boil again, simmer for 10 minutes, remove spices and put into jars. Cover with a disc soaked in whisky, brandy or similar alcohol, then cover with cellophane and tie up. Keep in a cool place.

Orange confiture *(Konfitura z pomarańcz)*

2 lb. sweet oranges   1 pint water for syrup
3 lb. sugar

Wash whole oranges and soak in cold water, covering them, for 24 hours. Pour off water. With fresh water cover oranges again, bring to the boil and simmer until they are soft, i.e. a wooden skewer can be inserted easily. Take out oranges, pour off water. Put sugar into preserving pan, add water and bring to the boil. Simmer this syrup for 15 minutes. It should thicken but not change colour. Cut each orange into 8 pieces, remove pips and simmer in syrup until oranges become transparent. This will take about 1 hour. Let cool and fill in small jars. Cover with cellophane and keep in a cool, dry place.

Rosehip confiture *(Konfitura z głogu)*

1 lb. rose hips (weighed $\frac{1}{2}$ pint water
after seeds have been   sugar
removed)

Collect hips after the first frost. Top and tail, slit open and remove seeds (these, when dried slowly, make an excellent tea) and add to boiling water. Simmer until hips are soft enough to be rubbed through sieve. Add 1 lb. sugar to 1 lb. pulp. Stir well and bring to the boil. Simmer until it sets. Put into small jars and cover with cellophane. Keep in a cool, dry place.

Drinks

Drinks and liqueurs play an important part in Polish hospitality. Wódka, the most widely known, is cheap and plentiful. It is drunk down in one gulp, not sipped. Drinks are made with it, but generally speaking it is drunk on its own.

In most households one can find home-made drinks, as alcohol, suitable for this purpose, is also very cheap. It would be a very poor hostess indeed who could not produce a bottle of Wisniak or Wisniovk, both made with Morello cherries. Most families have their own traditional recipe, based on the same ingredients, but with a slight difference.

Apple wine *(Wino z jabłek)*

6 lb. apples
2 lb. sugar
4 pints water

1 oz. yeast
2 oz. sultanas

Wash apples and cut away bad parts but do not peel or core. Mince and put pulp into a linen or muslin bag and squeeze out. Boil sugar and water and let cool. Cream yeast with a little of this liquid and add, as well as washed sultanas and apple juice, to syrup. Put into a stone or glass jar, cover with muslin and let it ferment for 6–7 weeks in a warm place. When no more bubbles appear, strain wine through filter paper, fill into clean, dry bottles and cork well.

Egg nogg *(Likier jajeczny)*

½ pint alcohol (brandy
or whisky)
1 vanilla pod

½ pint thin cream
8 oz. icing sugar
5 egg yolks

Put alcohol with vanilla pod, split lengthways, for 3–4 days in warm place, and cover container well. Bring cream to boil and whisk, having removed it from heat, with sugar and egg yolks for 20 minutes. Add to alcohol, whisking it together. Put into bottles and cork well. Leave vanilla pod inside. Although this drink can be used straight, away, it improves very much with keeping.

Plum liqueur *(Likier śliwkowy)*

2 lb. plums*   10 oz. sugar
3 pints wódka

* *The plums for this drink ought to be picked after the first frost.*

Wash plums and dry. Crush in a wooden bowl with the stones, i.e. leaving them in the plums. Add sugar and put into a large glass jar with a wide neck. Pour vodka over it and cover bottle. Put into a sunny position for 4 weeks. Strain through filter paper and put the liquid into small bottles. Cork and keep in a cool place.

Plum wódka *(Wódka ze śliwek)*

2 lb. dark blue plums 1 lb. sugar
1¼ pint water   1½ pints wódka

Halve plums, remove stones except for a handful which must be cracked open. Bring water and sugar to the boil, add plums and inside of cracked stones, let boil for a minute and allow to cool. Next day strain, measure liquid and, adding boiled cooled water, make quantity up to 1½ pints. Add wódka. Bottle and cork liquid and use after 2–3 months.

Wiśniak *(Wiśniak)*

    1 lb. morella cherries   1 pint brandy
    8 oz. sugar

Wash and stalk cherries. Stone and crack a handful of these. Discard rest of stones. Mince or chop cherries, put into large glass or earthenware jar, add inside of cracked stones as well as sugar. The kernel of cherry stones has a flavour similar to that of bitter almonds. Cover jar and let it stand for 4 weeks. Shake gently every day. Put into a preserving pan and heat to boiling point; do not let it boil but remove straight away. Allow to cool, add brandy, strain and bottle. Cork loosely at first and after a few weeks cork firmly and seal with wax.

The cherries should be kept after straining as they are excellent. They taste like cocktail cherries only as they are mashed they look different. They are valuable as an addition to drinks, stewed fruit, puddings, etc. but as they contain a fair amount of alcohol they should not be given to children. Kept in a screw topped jar, they will remain fresh for some time.

Cherry brandy *(Wiśniówka)*

    1 lb. morello cherries $1\frac{1}{4}$ pints water
    1 pint brandy   8 oz. sugar

Wash and stalk cherries. Put into a large jar and pour brandy over them. Close tightly and let stand for 10 days. Make syrup from water and sugar, simmering it for 5–7 minutes. Pour strained brandy into the *hot* syrup. Bottle and cork. It improves with keeping. Keep cherries for further use in screw top jar. They are excellent as cocktail cherries, cake decorations or an addition to fruit salads but do not give them to children as they contain alcohol.

Rosehip wine *(Wino z głogu)*

| 2 lb. rosehips* | 1 oz. sugar |
| 2½ pints water | 1½ oz. sultanas |

* *collect rosehips after first frost.*

Remove stalks and seeds from rosehips. Wash well, changing water several times. Bring 2 pints water and sugar to boil and let cool. Wash sultanas and either mash them in a mortar with pestle or mince. Warm ½ pint of water, pour over sultanas and put for 3 days in warm place. Put rosehips in a large glass jar or bottle and pour syrup over them. Cover lightly. After 3 days add sultanas and liquid. Cover jar with muslin and put in a warm place for 3 months. (The top of a kitchen cupboard is quite suitable.) Carefully pour into another jar, leaving sediment behind, and allow to stand for another 2 months.

Bottle wine, cork and seal. Place bottles horizontally in a cool dark place. This wine improves with age.

Mazagran

| ½ pint strong black coffee | 1 pint cold water |
| 2–3 oz. sugar to taste | 3 tablespoons brandy |

Add sugar to hot coffee to dissolve. Let cool. Add water and brandy, and allow at least 1 hour in refrigerator. Serve in tall glasses and add an ice cube to each glass. Drinking straws are used with this drink.

Sour milk drink *(Roztrzepaniec)*

| 1 pint sour milk | chives, finely chopped |

Whisk very cold sour milk with an egg whisk and add chives. This can be used as a very refreshing drink or served with hot, peeled potatoes. It is advisable to make only the amount to be consumed as it will not keep.

Iced sour milk *(Kwaśne mleko)*

This very refreshing drink is used in Poland the whole year round, but particularly in the summer. To go sour in the right way naturally, the milk must be unpasteurized. As unpasteurized milk is not obtainable in this country, we must use a different method; besides the milk you need only a few spoonfuls of plain yoghourt.

Warm milk to blood heat and let it cool but do not put it into the refrigerator. Rinse a well-washed milk bottle with a little yoghourt and pour the cooled milk into it. Cover with muslin and stand the bottle in a warm place until sour. This takes between one and two days, according to the time of the year and the temperature in which it is kept. When sour, put it into the refrigerator and serve very cold.

Lithuanian krupnik *(Krupnik litewski)*

1 lb. honey	$\frac{1}{4}$ pod vanilla
1 pint water	grated nutmeg
3 cloves	$\frac{3}{4}$ pint wódka
$\frac{1}{2}$ stick cinnamon	

Bring honey and water to the boil, add spices and let boil up several times. Let cool. Before serving, strain, bring to boil again and slowly add wódka. Serve hot.

This is a strong hot drink, much appreciated during the winter. It is served in small cups, normally used for black coffee.

Index of Recipes

222

227

228

229